YOU'RE NOT TOO MUCH

INTENSIVE LIVES IN AN EXPANSIVE WORLD

By Leela Sinha, M.Div.

Produced in the United States of America

Portions of this book first appeared on websites including bodyofpleasure.com and in sermons preached by Leela Sinha, M.Div.

First Edition, 2016

Trade Paperback Edition
ISBN 978-0-9978181-0-9

Night Lion Press
Scarborough, Maine
www.yourenottoomuch.com

Cover Illustration by Martin Whitmore

for Andy Dolph

Contents

INTRODUCTION

Dear Readers,

This book has been a long time coming. When I began, I had no idea how big a project it would become.

I mean, I knew enough to be intimidated by the idea of "writing a book," and enough to do it anyway, but I really had no idea what I was taking on.

For one thing, I was high on pain meds for a back injury. For another, it was just a twinkle in my eye at first, an attempt to understand why so many things had gone wrong in my life.

I'd lost friends, lovers, partners, work…

I'd struggled to get clients for coaching and for massage. I'd wrestled with things that other people found easy.

I got bored easily; I rotated through hobbies; I was good at a lot of things but never seemed to stick with anything as long as Everyone Said I should.

In fact, Everyone Said a lot of things that didn't work for me.

Slowly, in the hazy immobilization that only a major medical issue can offer, I stopped saying "the common factor is you" and started asking, "but what IS the common factor, really?"

So this book came from me thinking my life was a disaster.

But it turned out there was a pattern.

And that pattern had a story.

And thus, the idea of intensives was born.

People like me were the ones, I realized, who were too much. These were my best people. They *were* my people. They were my lovers, they were my friends, and they were my clients.

Yes, lots of my best clients were power holders, were fierce, were sexually adventurous, were queer. Yes, lots of my best clients were innovators, were creatives, didn't take no for an answer. Yes, lots of my best clients were survivors—of trauma, of abuse, of tragedy, of all three.

But what really bound them—and me—together?

We shared something, some ineffable quality, some... intensiveness.

We were all *super* intense.

We were *intensives*.

The rest, as they say, is history.

I was utterly delighted to discover a language for this quality; I was even more thrilled to see the response I got as I started to put the ideas out on Facebook. Private and public messages, people thrilled that I'd put words to their experiences.

I needed a word for the not-intense people; I chose *expansives*.

And as soon as I put two ends on the continuum, it became clear why I clicked with some people and not with others. It became clear almost immediately who this work would was going to resonate with and who it wouldn't.

Mostly.

The really squished intensives sometimes surprise me. I don't always know who is going to emerge from the sea of faces to ask, in a private moment or email, if I might be able to talk because, they say quietly, *they think they're intensive but they're not sure.* Sure, I'll say to a friend, let's get on the phone. And almost always, they're right. Intensive, squished almost beyond recognition.

It was our need to be seen, validated, visible—to be given permission to exist—that drove me from a few blog entries and a Facebook post or two to more posts, to more entries, to the wandering question sometime in May: *I wonder how many words I've written about this?*

After realizing I had half a book, I made the decision to write the rest.

I've been wanting to write a book, it almost didn't matter what, for years. I have a novel in progress, a few novel ideas lying in wait, and at least one other nonfiction book in progress... This one jumped the queue.

Why?

Because it is needed. Not in a theoretical, probably-maybe-helpful-to-someone way (though one of my novels does have an ulterior motive) but in a concrete, people-are-in-tears-from-my-Facebook-posts kind of way.

People whose breakups are peppered with "I can't take you anymore." People whose parents finally said, "I can't handle you, go play by yourself." People whose jobs and social lives were a series of shipwrecks foundering on the reefs and rocks of "you're too much."

These, I realized, are my people. And we need each other. I need them as much as they need me. I need clients and friends and colleagues who embrace my from-the-gut decision making and my wild interdisciplinary inspirations. I need clients who work like I do, all-in for a short burst, and then out. What Everyone Says doesn't work for me. I can't do what Everyone Says, because it turns out that for me, and apparently for lots of other folks, Everyone is wrong.

And it had to be said.

But then I began to wonder: How could Everyone be so completely off track for so many of us for so long? How did that even *happen*?

The resulting dive into world history turned up, along with everything else, the roots of a lot of racism. Everyone had been wrong about a lot more than I thought, and for a lot longer, and with a lot more cultural support than I ever suspected.

And that had to be said as well.

The result is in your hands.

This book defines intensives and expansives, explains the bias against intensives, and then talks about how intensives operate in our personal lives, in our work lives, in leadership, and in the world.

I keep producing more material, more than I could possibly fit in this book. I've had to start a Patreon (Patreon.com/leelas) to take the overflow. Every question leads to more thoughts, more connections, more answers.

My hope is that you will read this and see yourself or someone you love, that you will understand yourself and that person better, and that it will make your life more beautiful, richer, easier.

If you are an expansive, I hope this will help explain some of the people you know, and make them less confusing and frustrating. I hope you will be able to make sense of their choices and their style, and that you will be able to extend understanding and support, even as you are better able to explain yourself to them, and get their understanding.

I refer often to my own experience, but you should not think for a minute that mine is the only data from which I draw. I share other people's stories only when I have permission to do so.

And finally: If you have been dumped, fired, rejected, sneered at, or exiled for your intensiveness, I hope you can feel some comfort here, and I hope you find your people.

We are your people, and you are home.

Leela Sinha
May 2016

DISCLAIMER

Leela Sinha is not a medical doctor or licensed mental health professional. The information in this book, including but not limited to text, graphics, images and other material, is for informational purposes only. This book and the information herein is not intended to be a substitute for professional medical advice, diagnosis or treatment. Always seek the advice of your physician or other qualified health care provider with any questions you may have regarding a medical condition or treatment and before undertaking a new health care regimen, and never disregard professional medical advice or delay in seeking it because of something you have read here.

Leela Sinha and Night Lion Press do not recommend or endorse any specific tests, physicians, professional practitioners, products, procedures, opinions or other information that may be mentioned in this book or its related website. Reliance on any information appearing here is solely at your own risk.

PART ONE

UNDERSTANDING INTENSIVENESS

A Note to Expansives: Thank You

Dear Expansives,

We love you.

Even when you make us absolutely crazy.

Even when we are angry or withdrawn or impatient, we love you.

We love your calm presence, your steady support, your reminders to look before we leap.

That doesn't mean we will *take* your perfectly sensible advice. We just aren't like that. But it's not disrespect, it's not disregard—it's just that we function differently.

We know we can bend the facts to say anything we want. We can argue any lost case until it seems watertight. So we don't trust logic any more than we trust statistics.

We trust gut, which we know you find suspicious and unstable and ungrounded.

If we are ungrounded, you are absolutely right. But when we *are* grounded, our well-grounded guts are the solidest sources of information for a thousand miles.

Which is why we're such incredible *divas*. Yes, we insist on just-this-toothpaste and just-that-alarm—we spend ridiculous amounts of money on the things that matter to us, whether it's thousand-thread-count sheets or a camping toothbrush we're going to hack the handle off of to shave ounces. Because it keeps us grounded. Which keeps our guts in top shape, which allows us to feel like we know what's going on, to feel safe and secure in an incessantly changing world. We're not doing it to be pains in the ass, or even because we're spoiled. We're doing it because, for us, it's fundamental to giving you—and the world—our best.

We are passionate about giving our best.

And we are grateful to you for helping us make that possible. Truthfully, we hope we're doing the same for you, but we can't really even imagine what that looks like for you.

We light the fires. We know you tend them, you clear the fire circles, you gather the firewood. We build them. We light them. And then we walk away. And you keep them burning. We love to play with matches. We're not so good at keeping the flames going. Thank you for making our work last. Thank you for helping our work last long enough to matter.

We are passionate about making a difference.

Thank you for being the second CEO, the one who reorganizes the startup chaos into something that will live on.

Thank you for being the partner who supports our crazy ideas even when you don't understand them.

Thank you for being the friend who picks us up and dusts us off after we crash over and over again, just so we can find the magic that lets us build a technology that flies or find a relationship that works.

Thank you.

Thank you for keeping the home fires burning.

We need you to come home to.

Thank you.

Love,

Your inexplicable, beloved intensives

1 — 1
WHAT IS AN INTENSIVE?

An intensive is someone who is intense.

Our first clue that that's who we are usually comes from outside us, from the world.

"You're too much," people tell us.

"Don't you think you should tone it down?"

"You're going to need to back off a little if you want people to take you seriously."

An intensive tends to work hard and fast and then take a break.

An intensive makes friends by getting to know everything about you right away.

An intensive tends to go on to the next thing just before the thing they're doing is complete.

An intensive shoots for excellence if they care at all about the outcome. If they don't care, they probably won't do it at all.

An intensive isn't satisfied with a good enough relationship or good enough results or a job that just pays the bills. An intensive wants passion, pleasure, adventure, and transformation. Stability is a good sideline.

Their lovemaking is fierce and hot.

Intensives are the hare in the fable of the tortoise and the hare, and cultural stories have been telling us we're wrong for years.

We're not wrong. We're different.

Sometimes you need the hare. Sometimes you need the sprint. Sometimes you need the speed and intensity…and maybe an alarm clock…and a nap afterward won't hurt a thing.

We are the hares. It's okay for us to be the hares. The world needs us, too.

Intensives work like mad on a project and then rest like the dead, and then take on another project and then rest like the dead. We are either very passionate or totally uninterested in whatever is at hand. We make friends instantly and stay friends for a very long time. We tend to be entrepreneurs, founders, inventors, and CEOs. And sometimes ministers. And when the world doesn't work for us, we don't change—we set about changing the world.

If you're not an intensive, you're an expansive. So what does that mean?

Expansives are the tortoise in the story. Expansives are methodical and consistent. They do a little at a time, each day, and eventually they finish even the largest task. They prefer things calm and predictable. They are warm and welcoming and mostly really delighted to have people gather in the kitchen and talk about their days. They gather information slowly, and come to a decision based on that information. They find pro/con lists helpful. They rarely get really excited or really despondent unless they have complicating factors, like depression or trauma history. Expansives are the tenders of our world.

Intensives set things in motion. Expansives keep them going. Intensives like risks. Expansives uphold safety.

(In general.)

Of course, expansives and intensives are not rigid categories.

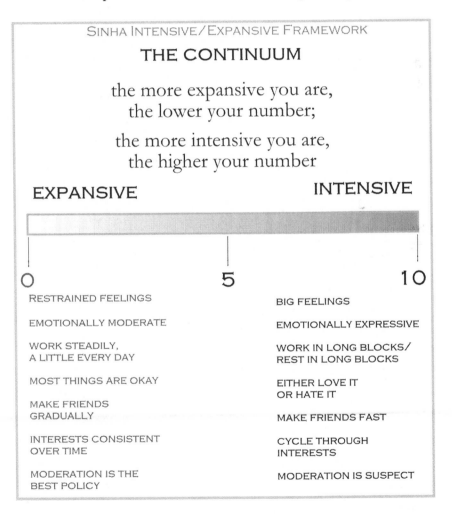

SINHA INTENSIVE/EXPANSIVE FRAMEWORK

THE CONTINUUM

the more expansive you are,
the lower your number;

the more intensive you are,
the higher your number

EXPANSIVE   **INTENSIVE**

0   5   10

EXPANSIVE	INTENSIVE
RESTRAINED FEELINGS	BIG FEELINGS
EMOTIONALLY MODERATE	EMOTIONALLY EXPRESSIVE
WORK STEADILY, A LITTLE EVERY DAY	WORK IN LONG BLOCKS/ REST IN LONG BLOCKS
MOST THINGS ARE OKAY	EITHER LOVE IT OR HATE IT
MAKE FRIENDS GRADUALLY	MAKE FRIENDS FAST
INTERESTS CONSISTENT OVER TIME	CYCLE THROUGH INTERESTS
MODERATION IS THE BEST POLICY	MODERATION IS SUSPECT

It's a continuum:

At the zero end, we have the most expansive people ever. At the ten end, we have the most intensive people ever.

Most of us fall in the middle somewhere (even me; I'm a nine).

The basic principle of this kind of system is that you can have some but not all of the characteristics of your type and still be that type. The odds are good that you will have one or two things from the *other* type's characteristic list. You're still legit.

Why the focus on intensives?

Like most category definitions, the idea of intensives and expansives as groups of people with shared characteristics emerged from the minority perspective. Expansives have not needed to define themselves because they are in the majority. My guess is that expansives make up about 70 percent of the population and about 90 percent of dominant cultural spaces. But intensives spend a lot of time being told that we are wrong. Naming helps fix that. It makes us ourselves instead of just the opposite of someone's definition of normal. It creates companionship and balance. It offers the chance for equality.

But expansives matter a lot; the expansive experience matters a lot. And if you're an expansive immersed in an intensive environment, you can face a lot of the same feelings and challenges—of being wrong, of not fitting in, of exhausting yourself maneuvering to try to be different.

So here's a quiz to see where you might fall. Take it, then read the descriptions and see how accurate you think the test is. It's an imperfect instrument. The Sinha Intensives/Expansives Framework is a way for us to understand ourselves in community and in the world.

1 – 2

THE SINHA INTENSIVE/EXPANSIVE FRAMEWORK TEST

Each question is yes/no binary, maybe is not an option. Do your best to answer as your essential nature, your gut reaction, not the thing you do because you were taught to do it.

1. Sometimes I get really loud and excited and talk fast.

2. I get impatient when people can't keep up with me.

3. If someone gets too excited, it can be overwhelming.

4. Passion leads to poor choices.

5. I prefer instructions to improvisation.

6. When I'm working on a project I might forget to eat.

7. slow and steady wins the race

8. the best way to change the world is through persistent, clear discourse.

9. People take too many chances.

10. I usually think I'm right.

11. Hard work and dedication are the keys to success.

12. When I'm working on a project I like to be able to focus completely on that project.

13. it's important to show up every day.

14. People sometimes think I don't care about things because I'm calm.

15. I like pro/con lists for decision making.

16. I think I'm often the most rational person in the room.

17. Messes show me unexpected interrelationships between things.

18. I like power.

19. If something is worth doing, it's worth doing 110%.

20. I am passionate.

21. When I cook, I lay out all the ingredients ahead of time.

22. People say I'm overwhelming.

23. Sometimes I move too fast for people I work with.

24. When I argue I keep my voice down.

25. I like to be real.

26. Sometimes my ideas make no sense to anyone else.

27. I like my life without too many big ups and downs.

28. I need to hold back around others.

29. When I start a big project I like to put all the stages on my calendar so I have a schedule to follow.

30. "Those who say it cannot be done should not interrupt the person doing it."

Scoring:

Add up your yeses for numbers 1, 2, 6, 10, 12, 17, 18, 19, 20, 22, 23, 25, 26, 28, 30. We'll call this group A.

Add up your yeses for numbers 3, 4, 5, 7, 8, 9, 11, 13, 14, 15, 16, 21, 24, 27, 29. We'll call this group B.

If A is bigger, you're probably intensive.

If B is bigger you're probably expansive.

(For the full-length, computer-scored test that will give you a 0-10 score, please visit http://yourenottoomuch.com/assessment/.)

1 – 3

ON TOLERANCE
AND BEING SQUISHED

Intensives and expansives come in two varieties: high tolerance and low tolerance.

Tolerance is about how comfortable you are with the *other* way of being.

High-tolerance intensives don't mind the slow, methodical pace of the expansives. High-tolerance expansives don't mind the fast, unpredictable pace of intensives.

Tolerance comes from a combination of exposure and temperament.

If you're an expansive who grew up in an intensive family or an intensive who works in a highly expansive field, you might have adapted to the point where it feels more comfortable for you to be in that environment.

You may also have adapted to the point where you feel like you have to *be* the way they are. That leads to squished intensives and fried expansives.

More on that later.

But if you held on to your own identity and you didn't go crazy, then you might have gotten really, *really* good at being around people who are not like you.

That might be delightful. And it definitely means you have choices.

It also means that you are incredibly valuable as a cultural translator. Unlike many of us, you can move fluidly between the worlds; you have your native space that you understand intuitively, and you have the environment you're most accustomed to—both.

Intensives and expansives often have trouble connecting; you are the person who can facilitate it. In leadership, you're the person who can connect the intensive leader to the expansive community or vice versa. *If* you want to. Does it light you up to do that? What is your fondest wish or greatest dream about it? What brings you joy?

Now there's a thing you should know about this. If you grow up with too much pressure to be expansive, then, even if you're intensive, you might show up as an expansive by the time you reach adulthood. It's hard to argue with something that surrounds you so thoroughly that you can't imagine anything else. Ani DiFranco sang, "You are subtle as a windowpane, standing in my view. I will wait for it to rain so that I can see you. It's like fish in the water who don't know that they are wet."

When you've been so thoroughly surrounded for so long, you may eventually discover, much to your surprise, that you're not an expansive at all, even though you've worked all your life to be one.

You're a squished intensive.

Squished intensives are intensives who have been forced into an expansive mold, despite all their intensive qualities. This could have happened with an expansive parent or family or school or job, although usually it happens well before adulthood. A squished intensive doesn't know they're an intensive. They know they try really hard to fit in. Life takes effort. And discipline. They often turn to drugs or alcohol to help them cope after a while, because it's a hell of a lot of work to pretend your energy is nice and sleek and smooth and even, when it's not.

As a result, squished intensives often end up being *very* rigid about following the rules and Doing The Right (expansive) Thing. They are smart and strong and powerful, and all that smart strong power is aimed at keeping them and everyone around them in the box that the expansive culture has provided.

It generally creates resentment and eventually anger, and possibly violence, either outward or inward (as depression).

The process of self-discovery is one of transformation. It can be uncomfortable, especially for the people around you who are not expecting you to change so radically and are "relying" on you to keep doing the Things You Are Supposed To Do (i.e., acting expansive). Embracing your intensiveness can come with a huge release and a lot of emotional baggage, but it's well worth it for your health and happiness.

Of course, squished intensives are one side of the spectrum. The other side is fried expansives.

A fried expansive is in an intensive career or family or relationship and has been trying to be intensive to fit in and function—and just keeps. Being. Tired.

That fatigue eventually becomes resentment and burnout.

For fried expansives, the process of self-discovery is mostly one of transformation and relief. It can be agitating for people around you who are expecting you to keep being intense. They may even feel that they've been *more* than accommodating already by going *so slowly* for you.

The truth is, you're going at exactly *your* pace now; they have to adjust to the pace that works for you. You can stop feeling like you're never caught up and they can go keep themselves busy (they should read the chapter on leadership) while you work at your pace.

If you're an expansive, you're probably reading this because someone you know or love is an intensive, or you're a brain geek. You probably are starting to see the patterns and wonder who you might know who fits with them, and you're wondering if this book can help you with the intensives in your life.

Yes, and yes.

Thank you for being here.

If you're an intensive, you probably just recognized yourself with that combination of fear and excitement that means that something interesting is about to happen.

Now what?

First, breathe a sigh of relief. *There is nothing wrong with you.*

I'm gonna repeat that: There is *nothing* wrong with you. (Although lots of people probably have told you that there is.)

You are an intensive. It's like having blue eyes or brown hair. You can change your appearance with effort, but it doesn't come easy. Being intensive is unusual, but totally normal. We're a minority, but we're an *awesome* minority. Welcome to a club where you actually belong.

When you're with intensives (and just intensives), you don't have to worry about overwhelming people or being "too much." Once everyone relaxes, they will say what they mean and ask for what they want. They will act like you are totally normal and be relieved to see your power come out in full force. They will delight in fantastic food and celebrate your *big giant ideas*. They will be more likely to say "why not?" than to tell you to "be reasonable." Intensives are not reasonable. We are wild, open-hearted, open-souled dreamers. We love big. We are pretty damn comfortable with risk. We laugh loudly, a lot, and make unexpected connections between seemingly unrelated things. We get *super* excited about things. We iterate fast—try something and see how it works, then modify it—because we're too impatient to work for eons to get something right before we give it a shot. We make rough drafts with the intention of editing them. We expect people around us to have opinions and to express them.

We *love* life. We live it as richly as we can. We push life to the limits and then a little further.

There's an immediacy to intensiveness. We want things done right now… or sooner, maybe. We love to ride that first wave of interest, desire, obsession. And we know—we have learned from a lifetime of experience—that if we don't catch it now, it might fizzle and not return. We fall in love with everything, not just with people. We fall in love with our hobbies and our curiosities and the immense beauty of the world and the possibility of changing it into something even better. We fall in love with what we see *could* be—we see possible futures and we want all the good ones to happen. We can't really accept a choice between possible positive results, and we don't want to say no—to ourselves, to our loved ones, to the world.

So we want to do it all, and we want to do it right away. Is it surprising, then, that we tend to be late all the time and thrice-over-committed? We just want to have fun, and save the world, and be the best at everything. All at once, please, and right now. Not later, not when we've sensibly planned it out and accounted for all contingencies—because we know that *later* rarely happens. We take the road and the road and the road and (as Robert Frost would have it) *knowing how way leads on to way,* we're pretty sure that by the time we've finished planning for this, our energy will be on to something else. So we have to live more immediately than most of the people around us, in constant *carpe diem* mode, ready to grab the next thing that comes flying down the line.

On the up side, it means we have some epic adventures. Before I was thirty-five I had lived in three countries without speaking the language in two of them, I had been to grad school and had completed a pile of other trainings, and I'd had three different career paths, all in traditionally male-dominated industries. Intensives are pretty good that way. We tend to take "no" as a challenge rather than an answer; one of our biggest tasks is to figure out when that's appropriate and when it's a violation of consent. That's not always clear, especially when you're dealing with institutions.

Some of us learn to temper our fierceness and leap-first-ness over time, because whatever else is in our lives requires that we do so. Some of us learn to lean on the focusing side, because that's what gives us a living, or what lets us craft the miracles we are accustomed to being responsible for.

We do take on the role of being responsible for miracles, which is a credit and a curse. When someone calls something impossible, we tend to answer with, "What if?" After a while, the groups and families and systems we're part of learn to rely on that. They throw down the gauntlet; we pick it up. Again, and again, and again. And if we don't watch ourselves, we can burn out. Being the knight in shining armor is awesome until you get sick or overwhelmed or tired or have a pet project of your own. If we haven't done our personal work, we get growly and grumpy and start acting like trolls under bridges.

That's why the personal work is so incredibly important for us. It's not optional. Because we live dialed to eleven, because we love intensely, because people tend to depend on us and we tend to be okay with that, because we are amazingly good at (at least) one thing—we can't afford to be spilling our emotional crap all over the floor. We get to *have* emotional crap, but when we blow, we tend to go sky-fucking-high and everyone gets hurt. So it's our responsibility, holding this fire hose of potential energy, to learn how to handle it. This is triply the case because we are disproportionately geeks raised by geeks and we may not know *how* to be gracious.

Also, we like to be honest. We have too much going on to lie about ourselves, unless we make that our full-time job.

And we're almost always up for adventure.

Welcome to a fabulous, interesting, engaging club.

So what to do? Study your brain like everything else. Learn what sets you off. Figure out what it is that makes you blow up. It's almost certainly *not* the thing you think it is. Learn about systems theory—it makes expansives and intensives alike make so much more sense. Get some therapy, just to understand yourself better. Play with neuropsychology a bit. Study change theory and game theory.

Even more than that, hang out with people. A lot. Get out into the soup and take risks, if that's not usually your thing. Take workshops. Take classes. Nothing like hands-on experience to really help you figure out what's going on.

The first time you notice the signals *before* you have your reaction, you'll be floored. The first time you have time to change your behavior based on that noticing, you'll be hooked. You will have your slips, but they will be few and far between, and it will feel less like "controlling your emotions" and more like "figuring out how to communicate how you feel so you get closer to what you want." The vulnerability ultimately feels safer than all the lying you used to do to try to get people not to feel bad.

When too many people tell us that we're out of our minds, we might start to agree with them—or at least stop verbalizing our ideas. That's a problem, like any squishing of the self is a problem.

Squishing ourselves is a problem because it can kill us. That kind of self-silencing leads to depression, and depression can be fatal.

Squishing ourselves is a problem because it can kill others. If we get mad enough and we don't kill ourselves, we might get very, very destructive.

Squishing ourselves is a problem because the world *needs* us. This, for me, is the most compelling reason on the list. (It says something about the number of years that I lived with depression. Don't judge.) The world *needs* outliers. It needs the extreme optimists and pessimists. It needs the outlandish possibilities. Sometimes, it actually needs our wild ideas, implemented exactly as we imagine them. But sometimes it's not the implementation of the absurdly extreme ideas that the world needs. Sometimes it's the *existence* of an idea that's way out there. Because that idea sets the boundary. If the most grandiose idea is moderate and not terribly daring, then the middle of the bell curve of people, opinions, and behavior will stay even more toward the center than that. But if the limit gets set *way out to sea*, then what might otherwise have looked outlandish looks reasonable by comparison. (This idea of a range of acceptable ideas is called the Overton Window).

When the AIDS crisis was gathering steam, a group formed called ACT-UP. They did radical, loud, outlandish, you-can't-do-*that* protests. They put AIDS activism on the map. They also established that the edges were *way* "out there" for both AIDS and LGBT activism. By comparison, almost everyone else looked "normal," "average," and "acceptable." That allowed AIDS justice work to get into the mainstream, because ACT-UP was illustrating just what not-mainstream would look like.

Intensives (and I bet ACT-UP had a lot of intensives, especially at the beginning) set that edge for everything. We say "why not?" We say "I dream of a world…" We say *"Fuck this shit*, I'm not going to take it anymore." We rewrite the rules. We ask the questions no one wants to speak aloud. We push the curtain all the way open so everyone has a full stage to play on. That's part of our *job*. That's who we are, that's part of why we are here. If you've ever gotten tired of being told, "You're outrageous, you think way too big. You have to be *realistic*," then you're exactly where you need to be, reading this book. We don't fit ourselves into reality; we fit reality to the future we want to be.

A Second Note to Expansives: How to Treat an Intensive

Dear Expansives,

We know you want to be nice to us. We know you love us. And we know we confuse you. Often. So here are some suggestions and explanations for what to do when we're immersed in a project or an idea, how to give us feedback, and why we might have acted in that really strange way just now. We promise, all this makes sense to us!

Mihaly Csíkszentmihályi introduced the concept of "flow states" in his 1975 research. He uses the idea of being carried along, as in a river, to describe absorption in work or a project to the point where the person becomes unaware of anything else. We do that a lot.

Please don't take our flow states personally. We will eventually emerge, disheveled and having forgotten to eat. Give us a chance to transition back into the real world before expecting us to be coherent. Know that the fact that we couldn't hear what you were saying for the last seventy-two hours has nothing to do with how we feel about you. We respect you. We care about what you have to say. We're just in a parallel universe.

Appreciate our enthusiasm. It's how we feel alive. We might or might not be *loud* about our enthusiasm, but it will be very present. "Fun" might be solving a math problem or scaling a rock wall or learning a new song from start to finish, including that really difficult riff right after the bridge.

Communicate kindly and directly. We are generally sensitive—our feelings can get hurt easily, but not by intensity. We *love* it when people have strong opinions. We don't love insulting opinions. We take things in intensely, too. If you put us down, we will probably remember it months later. If you give us kind and constructive feedback, we may well be delighted and run off to integrate it right away.

Get used to us responding fast—or not at all. If we want to do something, we will probably want to do it before some other interesting thing takes our focus, which means right away. We want to do the dishes for you—as long as we can do it right now—or we might need you to wait until we're done with the thing that has us in its thrall, after which we might forget entirely and need to be reminded. Please don't take it personally.

Don't interrupt us if you can possibly help it. Working in our own rhythms is very important to us. When we're focused on something, *that thing* gets our attention. If you ask us to interrupt that we may be willing to do it, but we may also be irritable and distracted because our brains just don't let go of what we were doing that fast.

Fall in love with who we are, not with who you wish we were. We might change, if something bothers us, on our own schedule—but not on yours. In fact, if you push us on something, we're likely to be resistant to the change even if it's something we were previously planning to do anyway. Unless we *ask* to be pushed. Then it was our idea. See how that works?

Appeal to our higher nature. We tend to have a highly idealized sense of self.

Regardless of how much data we like to crunch, our primary interest is in our gut. We *know* we're right. We have adjusted to chasing down the data to support that gut feeling, but only to indulge the world around us and to reassure us that we're not crazy.

Accept our outrageously high goals. Don't be patronizing: We can smell it a mile away and it stinks. Believe that we are capable of achieving those goals. Let us know, clearly and honestly, how much support we can expect from you—if that's zero, then say so. In either case, get out of the way!

Tell us what you need. We don't think like you do, so what you think is obvious is NOT obvious to us—and vice versa. You probably need to do things in a measured way, a little at a time.

Think of us as magical creatures traveling between this world and another. When we're working on a project we are in a different world, almost literally. We're in a parallel universe; we can see you but we might not be able to hear you, and our reality is phase-shifted just a little bit. We'll come back across the line when we can. We think of you as magical creatures who are anchored so firmly in this reality that you never get pulled out. We can't really imagine how that works, but it looks nice and stable. We're attracted to that rootedness, even if we can't live that way ourselves.

Love,

Your Intensives

1 – 5
THE INTENSIVE HERO

Intensives are relatively uncommon in our day-to-day world—probably (this is a guess) 30 percent, maybe less, of people in the United States. But intensives make great fictional heroes, because we have a habit of going off half-cocked (see how biased that language is? More on that later) and following our hearts instead of the rules.

Famous fictional intensives:

- Harry Potter, Hermione Granger, and Dumbledore from the *Harry Potter* series

- Ellie Arroway from *Contact*

- Gandalf, Frodo, and Aragorn from *The Lord of the Rings*

- Olivia Pope from *Scandal*

- Belle, her father, Lumière, and the Beast from Disney's *Beauty and the Beast*

- The Jinni from *The Golem and the Jinni*

- *Albert from* Bye Bye Birdie

- *The Phantom from* The Phantom of the Opera

- Ado Annie from *Oklahoma!*

- Harold Hill from *The Music Man*

- Alexander Hamilton (from history, and from the musical)

Famous fictional expansives:

- Ron Weasley from the *Harry Potter* series

- *The nurse in* Romeo and Juliet

- Ram's younger half-brother, the one who refuses to rule, in the *Ramayana*

- Snow White from Disney's *Snow White*

- Cogsworth and Mrs. Potts from Disney's *Beauty and the Beast*

- *The Golem from* The Golem and the Jinni

- *Rose from* Bye Bye Birdie

- Will from *Oklahoma!*

- Marian the Librarian from *The Music Man*

- *Merlin from* The Once and Future King

- Galadriel and Samwise Gamgee from *The Lord of the Rings*

- Aaron Burr (from history, and from the musical *Hamilton*)

Let's look a little more in depth at a couple of these.

Hermione Granger is an intensive's intensive. Why do I say that? Because if you're not an intensive she has a hard time connecting with you, especially in the earlier stories. Her impatience, certitude, and passion for knowing everything and being right are classic hallmarks of an intensive. Also, using that Time-Turner so she can literally take twice as many classes as usual? Intensive through and through.

Now, let's look at Frodo Baggins. He's a good hobbit but, unlike his uncle, he has that glint in his eye and an obsessive curiosity from the beginning. He's humble, but he's also adventuresome (a good hobbit is extremely expansive; it would be interested to consider how this intersects with British culture at the time and Tolkien's own character). He's likely to go with his gut rather than the rules. Samwise Gamgee, on the other hand, only goes with the Fellowship because he feels it's his duty to protect Frodo. He doesn't want to leave home. Adventuring is absolutely not his thing. He spends a great deal of time saying, "I'm not sure this is a good idea" and then scrambling to catch up. Classic expansive. He would prefer things tidy, safe, and clean.

Now look at Snow White. She's content. Intensives can be happy or sad or delighted or whatever, but we are rarely consistently *content*. She is happy to keep house for the Dwarves, live in the forest, and not think much beyond her fairly steady life. It takes the witch with the apple interrupting her routine for things to change and the adventure (and story) to begin. She's one of the very few main-character expansives out there.

Characters like Galadriel, Merlin, and Gandalf are a little trickier—their ancientness will have somewhat mellowed any external tendencies to intensiveness. Merlin is very laid-back, but he's also not afraid to make Wart uncomfortable. Gandalf does a lot of biding his time, but I get the sense that he feels impatient and is only biding because it's good strategy. He also has quite a temper.

Galadriel feels intensive, but certainly stays well out of the fray.

1 — 6

THE IMPACT OF
INTENSIVENESS

As an intensive, you're probably attracted to power.

You are probably also a little bit scared of having it. That's your expansive training. But you can't avoid it, because more than other people, it's IN you.

The truth is, intensiveness IS a kind of power, focused and channeled and sexy and gorgeous and dangerous.

And when we love it, we love ourselves.

And when we hate it, we are pushing away from something that has made us who we are—the horrors, the wild and unexpected successes, everything.

Intensiveness is how we got here.

It's also tripped us all up at least once, somehow.

Intensiveness gets you to do things you never thought you were capable of; it also gets you to push past your limits so you are injured or resentful or burned out. It gives you a charisma that gets people to believe you and follow you; it gives you the passion to have a vision for it. It also makes you less willing to see and do things any way but your way. It makes you stubborn, and makes it hard to be wrong—ever.

For better or for worse (usually both), it gets you to take huge risks.

Intensiveness helps you make wild leaps of logic and faith that generate unexpected and revolutionary work. It helps you make connections that no one else understands—*and* it leaves you standing alone if they fail.

Intensiveness builds a fabulous connection almost instantly with other intensives—*and* it makes some expansives look at you with equal parts admiration and fear as they back slowly away.

Intensiveness gets you to be more productive than anyone in a fifty-mile radius when you're on fire with an idea—*and* it gets you to lose interest 80 percent of the way into the project and go on to the next awesome thing. (I call this the "80 percent problem.")

So how do we lean into the good side and mitigate the bad side?

As a cartoon character from my childhood used to say, "Knowing is half the battle."

The other half is loving the hell out of your intensiveness.

That's what this book is for.

After learning all of this, many intensives start to recognize the ongoing friction with the expansives in their lives and start to wonder if it's at all possible for intensives to share space and love and jobs and life with expansives.

Yes. Absolutely. All the time. We love all kinds of people. There are lots of ways we can be ourselves and still not overwhelm people who aren't as intense as we are. Think of it like cooking heat: If your kitchen-stove dial goes from zero to ten, there's a best cooking temperature for each food.

As intensives, we're usually good at high heat—seven to ten on the scale. There are factors that modify our behavior, but under it all we're smoking oil, flambé, searing heat. Expansives are low, slow, and steady , more like cooking in a Crock-Pot. On the zero-to-ten scale, they're four and under. In the middle we have our lasagna, baked at 350 for 45 minutes. One isn't better than the others; they all have their advantages. But if you put a lasagna in a smoking-hot frying pan, it will burn. That's how we get into tension with expansives around us. What *should* be for them isn't what *should* be for us. We function differently, we thrive differently, and we live differently. And it's all perfect.

We can learn to do things like expansives occasionally, or we can change the rules so that they suit us, but we can't assume that How It Works For Them is How It Works For Us.

It just isn't true.

And that's okay.

1 – 7
MEDITATION FOR INTENSIVES

Although it seems like there should be things that we don't do, *ever*, there are no hard-and-fast rule. There are some things that are less likely (becoming a successful file clerk) but there's nothing that someone hasn't done, especially if they've been told they can't do it.

In general, we're not very good at sitting through long, pointless meetings, waiting for people to "get comfortable" with something, not flirting, eating dessert last. We like to plan a little (on the back of a napkin will do), be ready, and then *go!* Waiting after we're ready saps our energy and tends to lead to us being distracted or involved in something totally different by the time everyone else is ready.

So how do we manage when we want to try something that we're resistant to?

I've done this a few times. Once with cleaning my house. That's still a work in progress. And once with meditation—that's a more complete story.

For years, people told me I should meditate.

For years (okay, decades), I didn't think so.

Or, rather, I believed them. I agreed that I *should*, but I didn't think I wanted to, and therefore I didn't think I *would*.

Last year, something shifted, and I finally took up meditation for about six months. It was easy, it came naturally, and it ran its course. Six months isn't long enough to be a habit, but it's long enough to remember why I want to do it and it's long enough to remind me to choose it occasionally. After six or so months of consistent, daily meditation, it entered the rotation of things I do to get grounded. I no longer resist it and I no longer do it every day.

Unlike some other things and some other times, I decided to start easy and be very forgiving. This is a *great* tool if you want to do something you're resisting. Intensives are, more than others, driven by pleasure, and easy, successful experiences feed our brains the right chemistry. After all, meditation comes easy to me but it's something I've resisted basically my entire life, so why set myself up for failure?

I started with five or ten minutes. I used an app. Why not? I even let the nice lady on the recording talk me all the way through my first session. When she didn't show up in the second session I was a little surprised, but figured I knew what I was doing enough to make it work. I was right.

I indulge myself: I switch soundtracks, I do it when I feel like it, I do it every day when I want, I do it lying down. As I write this I'm on, the app tells me, a fourteen-day streak. Fabulous! Or I'm not! Fabulous!

And it's a total escape, an escape from the running around in my head that my thoughts do all the time.

I've noticed a few interesting things.

1. When I meditate I set a timer for twenty minutes, but I still mostly do my best, deepest meditation after the timer goes off. I'm finally starting to drop into it and I don't want to stop. Mostly I don't have to, so I just keep going.

2. When I do get into it, I can feel the energy (chi, prana) flowing in my body. There are specific sensations: a sense of warmth and light that starts in my root chakra and moves up, growing into a globe of light; really warm palms; a lightheadedness; that bubbling-over sense of pleasure that you get when you're utterly gleeful about something, only without the actual glee. It feels like I'm going to squeal or giggle or laugh with joy. It's pretty good.

3. Going back to that glow: I have a sense of myself as glowing from the inside.

4. When I get off track, I go back to following my breath and the chi comes with it and I'm back to that bubbling-over-joy thing in no time.

5. I like it. And then I wonder if I like it too much. And then I wonder if it's weird to actually like meditation. And then I wonder if I'm supposed to feel that good. And then I decide I don't care and go back to watching my breath.

And I notice this: When the bubbling-over-joy feeling and that glowing-from-the-inside thing come up, my first impulse is to close my throat and dim the light, keep it inside me, not let it outside the boundaries of my skin.

That suppressed bubbling up looked awfully familiar.

Kind of like a metaphor for the rest of my life or something.

It's not like I try to keep things from bubbling up and over or anything. It's not like I wrote a book about it…

Oh wait.

What in everloving hell was I doing?

I was doing what a lot of intensives do. I was trying to moderate my intensiveness. Lord knows why; there are a million possible life reasons. What matters was what I ended up doing—and, after I noticed it, the answer was: *not fucking that. (Ahem.)*

There are lots of soft, gentle, sweet, nonintense people in the world, and when they are soft and gentle and not intense in that way, they are beautiful. Just gorgeous. All starlight-glowy and comforting and easy. Absolutely perfect.

And there are places and times and ways that we intensives are gentle and soft and sweet, too. There are places and times and moments where just rocking someone in your arms while they cry is the most natural thing in the world, of course.

But here's the thing. When intensives try to cover up the light that's beaming out everywhere? That's not going to work. First of all, we're hiding under blackout curtains. So instead of making the bright light gentle, it just leaks out and makes weird shadows on the wall and hurts people's' eyes.

Secondly, when we are covered up completely, we are *boring*. We are *no fun*. We are awkward and uncertain and holding our breath and it is hot and stuffy under there.

Then, when we do come out, we sometimes make a big mess because we have *so much* pent-up energy.

No good.

Nope. We've got to be bright. We are made to be beacons, shining all that gorgeous light all around and all over the place. We spill like beautiful golden sunshine, we spill like silvery moonlight, we spread illumination like the first spotlight on a dark stage. And then we grow that light and everything around us gets a little glow on, too.

If you're trying not to be you, you're likely to end up a cardboard cutout with your face on the front.

And as intensives, we're fucking bright. It's how we're built. We need to shine. Even my meditation makes me shine brighter.

Go on. Get your shine on.

1 – 8

SELF-ACCEPTANCE

I went for a walk this morning. I couldn't help myself. It was glo-
riously bright and the sky was blue and the sun was at that low
slant we call "magic hour" because it is made of magic and possibility and it makes everything look beautiful.

It was that sky that called me first, then the bright yellow of the
second-wave maple trees, then the easy and inviting stretch of my
quiet little road. *Just to the end and back*, I told myself. *Just that.*
I turned off the washing machine (which needs babysitting) and
stuffed my hands in my fleece. *Just that.*

But when I got there, having taken pictures of the maples and their
companions, my feet carried me on, unbidden, across to the side-
walk and down the state route that connects my neighbors and me
to the world. Everything was glorious. I love mornings anyway, but
this was particularly one to savor. The houses were beautiful, the
trees were beautiful, the marsh was glistening navy-blue paths on a
straw-gold field in that early light.

In the end, it was wind that turned me around, wind and the fleece
that wasn't much proof against it. I've lived here three years and
some; I know that the wind that starts at the marsh builds to the

water's edge, and I've no desire to be miserable. I'm done with that.

So I wandered back, past the construction guys working over the train tracks, with the sun warm on my back. I listened to the rooster, who reminded me of biking to school in France with my ragg wool gloves to warm my fingers, and of watching the corn come up in magic, invisible rows that only appeared when they all lined up and then were gone again. I thought about France and Portugal and rising with the sun and saw my young neighbors on their way to school and finally I came home to babysit the washing machine, but, God, what a glorious day.

Now what does this have to do with intensives?

Truly, it's a classic case. Having a well-formed plan for my morning (write, then do three loads of laundry before the cable guy gets here), I tossed it out the window for walking around in sandals and a fleece on a sunny thirty-seven-degree morning, because the morning felt SOdamnGOOD. There are things you just can't pass up. I guess for some people that's whiskey or a marathon. For me it's the utter glory of a crisp October morning, laundry and cable guy be damned.

We are at our brilliant best when we give ourselves space and permission to live like this. We're good with responsibilities, but we will be best if we can give ourselves over to whatever is best in the moment. We can learn to cook by the book, but we are far better turned loose in a foreign farmer's market with a pocketful of cash and a hungry belly. You will not starve by us, I promise. If our gift is not food, we will tell you well in advance, but we will also know where the best food *is*.

We are at our best when our senses are not just sated but extravagantly catered to.

I officiated at an elegant backyard wedding this weekend, and the solarium there had a blooming miniature orange tree. It was utterly exquisite.

The scent of the tree mattered. It changed the whole experience of walking into that room. Spirits opened, senses soared…

All this works because we allow ourselves joy—intense, immense joy. If we don't, we can't give the best, either. When we don't give joy like that, we fail and we feel it. We are capable of focusing in on all the grief and sorrow and destruction in the world, and we can turn that into righteous anger which we can use to change the things that matter most to us, but the true truth is that when we work from rage we lose out on the power of healing and redemption. That becomes a problem over time, eating away at our insides, leading to fear, paranoia, exhaustion, and burnout.

When we allow ourselves soaring, boundless joy, the unconscionable disasters don't hurt any less, but they are survivable. And we are the ones most likely to be able to think beyond them to some other possibility, if we allow it.

We are best working from love and joy. They are the best fuel sources.

In the film *Monsters, Inc.*, the punch line (spoiler alert) is that there's much more energy in laughter than in tears.

That's not just a good bedtime story.

It's the truth.

In a way, this whole book is about self-acceptance. It's about understanding ourselves better so we can understand why we are the way we are and navigate the world better. That's a no-brainer.

Why is that so hard sometimes?

Well, it's hard to accept yourself when the world around you is telling you you're doing it wrong. Any marginalized group can tell you this story: all the racial and cultural minorities, introverts, GLBT people, any time "everyone knows that everyone does it" this way or that, there's someone doing it differently.

The world around us is designed for the majority, the expansives. We intensives take up a lot of space relative to our numbers—we tend to be power holders, entrepreneurs, CEOs, leaders, visionaries. But when you actually look at how many of us there are, it's probably a third or less of the total population. I'd love to see someone do a large-scale survey and figure it out for sure. But because we are not most of the people, we don't generally make the norms. Sometimes we get to make the rules, but what is considered "normal" comes from what is common. Expansives are everywhere.

So we have to build up a series of defenses for ourselves. Over time we learn to hide ourselves or dismiss the criticism of others, or both. Only by doing this can we continue to be ourselves. But even the best-defended person gets worn down after a while, frustrated and exhausted from that self-defense.

My clients regularly say to me, "You mean I can just do it the way I want to?"

And I say, "YES. You can do it the way you want to. Please do."

For example: Recently I read a book. That's not unusual. But I read it all in one day, with only a few breaks for food and a webinar at lunchtime. It was for work, related to the coaching I do, but it was a popular book, easily accessible. At the end of the day I was bleary-eyed, the kitchen looked like a tornado had hit it, and I wanted to think about nothing important for at least twenty-four hours.

I used to beat myself up for doing things like that. I used to feel like I should have done XYZ differently, kept the kitchen clean, whatever.

Now I know that this is just how I work best, in four- or eight-hour blocks. I like to set my sights on something and really dig in deep, follow the rabbit hole all the way to the bottle and the cake marked Eat Me and Drink Me. And then eat and drink. It might take me a week or a month to come out of my little adventure, but that's the best way for me to get things done.

Increasingly, I'm learning to set up my life so that can happen, creating large blocks of time when I plan to do big things. If people come over while I'm down a rabbit hole, then they come over while I'm down a rabbit hole. The floor isn't vacuumed and the dishes aren't done because I'm busy. I'm one person and I am choosing to use my energy efficiently instead of on social acceptability.

When we learn to do this, we become productivity powerhouses. I *will* clean my house—probably a couple of days after a work binge. Everything gets reset, the trash gets taken out, the cables get coiled.

I might even get a haircut.

Everything gets done, just not the way everyone else does it. We learn. Over time we learn to trust our own rhythms.

Because if we don't, we are perennially frustrated. An hour on most projects is just enough time to get started, to really start to roll. I get things done in the first hour, but I don't really hit my stride until ninety minutes or more. That's not wrong. It's not bad. It just requires a different kind of space for working than the multitasking, constant interruption of the usual office.

We often need things just so, too. Usually I put my computer *here*. Today I'm putting it *there* because the usual spot feels…off. Icky. Do I sound like a diva? Lots of divas are intensives. But we are so sensitive to our environments that, while we *can* get things done under irritating conditions, we are worlds better if we can eliminate the irritation without judgment about the fact that we want it eliminated.

That precision can stop us from getting started (oh, I need perfect conditions or why bother?) but it can also lead us to try for bigger and bolder goals than we would otherwise consider. (*What if I reorganize the whole room so I can always sit by the window? What if I had a whole office to myself? What if I hire childcare so I can work uninterrupted for six hours every day?*) We get the idea that we need it to be just like this or that, so we go after it and accept no substitutes.

The place where this can trip us up (one of them) is when we need the halfway stage so we can see how to get to the finish line.

Danielle LaPorte is a powerful personality—a thinker, a writer, a speaker, formerly a coach. I believe she is also an intensive. She once wrote an essay about getting rid of the ugly furniture you don't like and living with the bare floor until you can get the thing you want, to make energetic space for the right thing. Sometimes that's great advice. But sometimes you need to buy the halfway thing, to get yourself from your college futon to a cheap sofa just so you can begin to imagine that you're the kind of person who has a sofa in their living room. From there, you can start to imagine the luxury feather-pillow couch or the vintage re-upholstered fainting couch or whatever you've been dreaming of. Halfway might be an important step. We tend to deny ourselves halfway.

Sometimes that denial is important, because one of my talents is making "good enough" work for far too long. This goes for all kinds of things, not just furniture.

But sometimes it just makes our lives harder. Or makes us live entirely in a hoped-for future in our heads.

Self-acceptance means lots of things.

- It means letting the way we do things best be the way

we do things.

- It means wanting what we want.

- It means surrounding ourselves with people who love us the way we are.

- It means taking responsibility for changing ourselves when something needs to be changed.

- It means allowing today's reality to be the reality we have, and allowing tomorrow's reality to be the project we're working on.

- It means not beating up on ourselves for not having made tomorrow into today by last week.

We are so good at creating things that we tend to expect ourselves to make it happen now if not sooner. While there is a great deal we can change, some of it comes with far too high a cost. Figuring out how to go with *what is* while working toward the future opens up a lot more space. When you're not disappointed in yourself, you can actually think about how to take the next steps.

The advanced course, after self-acceptance, is self-celebration. This is best undertaken in the company of other intensives.

Imagine you're planning a project. In a room full of intensives, you stand up and talk about your plans. You talk about the way it will go at first, how you will expand nationwide, and then the prospects for spreading the work to France.

Someone stands up and says, "Hey, I think you might want to consider the UK first, because…" Someone else says, "Have you considered Australia? I've got contacts there and I've got a really good feeling about Australia." That sounds good to you, so you ask if they can put you in touch.

In a room full of expansives, people would have told you to slow down, do some more analysis, maybe take a year to fully understand the process. "And have you considered the dangers? And…"

Now, you might need to do a little plan-checking before you actually *plan* the trip to Australia, but yeah, you did think about that stuff. And the trouble is that if you slow down that much, the momentum will be gone.

The bigger problem is this: Logic can be tweaked to say anything you want it to say. Only guts tell the truth, and your gut says this could be big if you can get the momentum you need.

Your gut is processing all the data from everywhere.

And the idea *feels good*.

You have learned to follow what feels good. Because what feels right generally *is* right. Discernment between what feels like a quick fix and what feels like a long-term pleasure is a honed skill, and you have honed it. Learning and practicing tracking those feelings in your chest and belly has led to a whole other way of approaching plans and problems.

Of course you consider the logic. But you also know now to prioritize the feeling.

Getting into a room full of intensives to make your decisions is a celebration of your intensiveness, of the brilliance of your system, of the way you are wired.

The more you live like this, the closer you get to pleasure and ease all the time.

This is what self-celebration, self-trust, living fully as an intensive is all about. This i what it means to be an intensive.

Give your gifts to the world. It needs them.

Be yourself so you can access your gifts.

1 – 9

IT DOESN'T HAVE TO BE HARD

S ometimes—you never know—your gifts might even extend to things like the Shoulds: exercise, cooking, housecleaning, the stuff you tend to blow off because it's not your passion and it's not as much fun. We have an easy time ignoring the things that don't appeal to us. But the trick is not to force it.

The trick is to make it *appealing*. Pleasure is at the heart of your motivation. Allow your rationalization skills full scope and see what happens. Everyone's different—some of these may be easy for you already. But some are probably not.

The tasks you don't do easily and naturally—that's what we're talking about here. But maybe you can make them easy and natural, if you do them *your* way.

Take **exercise.** Either you make yourself do it every day and become a triathelete, or you do it for a week and then stop, and then. six months later, do it for a week…and so on.

Here's what's at play.

Perfectionism is the biggest mood-killer here. You know you *should* exercise for an hour four days a week. (See the Should there?) But today you have some reason why you can't exercise for an hour. So it's not worth bothering. You know you *should* run, but you're getting over a back injury, so instead of walking or biking, you don't do anything. *Ideally* you would ride your bike to the beach, but your bike is missing a part, so instead of walking (to the beach or somewhere else), you do nothing.

As an intensive, you want to do it *right*, all the way, all the time. Anything less feels unsatisfying. You don't get that "Yeah, I did it!" burst from the halfway mark. So you skip it.

Easy distraction is another one. After the startup phase (buy the stuff! learn the things! do the research!), most exercise falls into a fairly predictable routine. So then you start looking for excuses not to do it and looking for a different thing to do instead, because the startup phase is interesting and engaging and full of hope. The doing-it phase is just doing it.

Learning orientation is related to easy distraction. As intensives, we want to keep learning and growing; our brains need to be engaged. Things that become routine, like running, stop being engaging.

So what do you do?

1. Get over your perfectionism. This is easier said than done, and it takes practice, but it's well worth it. Pick something you *know* you aren't good at but that you enjoy, and do it regularly until being bad at something doesn't feel so weird. Let yourself be bad at it. Let yourself just enjoy it. Learn that no one is watching, and stop caring if they are. The only way you learn this is by practicing it, so get out there and do something (anything! doesn't have to be exercise!) that you enjoy being bad at.

2. Pick the right sport. Or the right distraction. The "right sport" would be one that requires your constant attention. Rock climbing and surfing work well for me: They require 100 percent focus. In my case, there's also pretty much no excuse—there are two rock gyms in my area and the beach is right down the street. Look for activities that have you interact with the elements or with other people—something unpredictable. You want to keep the puzzle-solving part of your brain happy. Alternatively, pick something unengaging, like running, and then pick a distraction, like podcasts. With the right distraction, you can do almost anything and not be bored out of your skull. You may want to combine these:, run with a podcast half the week, the other half go to the rock gym.

3. Finally, even though we have to live with it sometimes, we hate doing things halfway. We're not wired for it. It bugs us. We resist it. We tend to not do it at all instead of compromising. That means you should plan to exercise every day, or every weekday, as consistently as possible. Create a structure that allows you to avoid *halfway*—do not break the routine, do not look for ways to have two routines. Our ability to be ultrafocused means that single routines are better. Get up, get dressed, go work out. Or finish the workday, change in the washroom, go to the gym. Or you may need to change it up to persist. Give yourself the experience of freedom, do it whenever, let everything count. Total amnesty is yours. Find the system that works for you.

Also, tell yourself, "I'm the kind of person who…" and see what else that changes, or what other stories you have about those kinds of people. You might find a clue to your resistance.

Now, if you *love* your sport and you're totally dedicated to being an athlete, this will not be a problem for you. Exercise is just an example. Let's look at another example.

Cooking.

Again with the perfectionism and the easy distraction.

Allow yourself some shortcuts. Some days you will pour a jar of curry sauce over a package of chicken tenders and simmer them for 20 minutes, and that will be dinner. That's actually *just fine.* Throw a handful of prewashed greens on the plate with a tablespoon of decent salad dressing and call it good.

Change it up. Shop according to what looks good at the store, not a strict list. YouTube is your friend—it will teach you what to do with almost anything you buy.

Always have a frozen pizza at the ready. Some days your experiments will fail. That has to be okay. To make it okay, have a quick and easy backup plan.

Cook for a crowd, even if you don't have a crowd, and freeze the leftovers in single portions. You can also freeze the leftover ingredients in single portions so you can make single servings later. If you're cooking for one, experimenting can be a very low-stakes experience.

Cook what you love. Don't make food you're *supposed* to like until you're in the habit of cooking regularly. Make food you *do* like, and buy the rest premade.

Keep your kitchen clean(ish). If you can't find the counters, you won't cook, almost guaranteed. Organize, tidy, and give away food you haven't opened in a year (it seemed like a good idea at the time).

Housecleaning.

Get over your perfectionism. I cannot say this enough. Doing half the dishes is better than doing none of them, trust me. Vacuuming one room (the one where you store the vacuum) is better than no vacuuming at all. Doing two loads of laundry is better than going without T-shirts and underwear. Do half or a quarter or even a tiny fraction of one job, just to break the inertia. Sometimes I just wash all the silverware. Five hours later, I get to the bowls. Then the plates. Then the pots on the stove don't look so bad. You get the idea.

Keep your promises to yourself. If you promise yourself you only have to do the silverware, don't move the goalpost. Stick with the silverware and congratulate yourself on a job well done.

Figure out how you clean and work with it, not against it. I clean in a random-looking, haphazard way. I do a few dishes, go to the table to get some more dishes, realize there's trash on the table, pick up and throw away the trash, realize the trash needs to go out, take the trash out, take the recycling out, grab a cup on my way through the living room, and go back to the dish sink. The disadvantage to this is that it takes a while to look like I've made any progress. The advantage to this is that when I finish, everything has been attended to, at least a little bit.

Talk to someone. We're easily distracted, which means we're ripe for getting off the cleaning track entirely. Get a friend on the phone and tell them their job is to keep you distracted so you keep cleaning. If a friend isn't available, maybe a podcast will help. Failing that, put on some music and boogie around as you clean.

Part of self-acceptance is setting thresholds of *enoughness.* Coach Jennifer Louden has been talking about "conditions of enoughness" for years. While a House Beautiful home would be ideal, what does "clean enough" look like? Set a couple of thresholds.

Do not clean in a mad frenzy right before someone comes over. I mean, you can if you must. But try to make cleaning something you do at your leisure and for yourself, because you enjoy the result. For bonus points, take the time to enjoy the process. Treat it like a craft. Light incense or a candle, and use that intensive-ultrafocus superpower to work on each thing in turn. Clean the dishes, then clean out the sink trap, then wash the sink itself. Then the counter on the left. Then the counter on the right. Take each step in turn.

Accept your priorities. Intensives do what we want to do fiercely and deprioritize everything else. It's how we are. So figure out what is keeping you from doing something, even if it seems like it shouldn't be. For example: I will not lift a lid to use a hamper. I just won't. I've tried to get myself to do it and it never happens. So either I need a step-lid hamper or I need a hamper without a lid. I don't try to convince myself that I will change my ways. I figure out where my dirty clothes accumulate (in the bathroom) and I put a hamper there. Without a lid. When I lived in a different house, my clothes piled up in the living room right outside the bathroom. Eventually I figured it out and tucked a pretty basket under the coffee table as a hamper. Find solutions that fit *you*; stop wearing yourself out trying to fit yourself to the solutions.

Know when to stop. Allow yourself to stop when you start to feel tired. Don't push yourself into misery, or you'll learn that cleaning equals misery and you'll never want to clean. Leave yourself enough energy to go out dancing. You deserve it.

I grew up in New England. We've got a thing here—that hard is better than easy. As a culture, as a region, we tend to behave like there's something special about you if you did it in the hardest way possible.

It took me a long time to get over that.

Whatever you're doing—some individual task, studying, playing, climbing a mountain, writing a book—it doesn't have to be hard. There's no virtue in working harder.

1 — 10
STRUGGLE IS NOT A VIRTUE

Let's look at the valorization of struggle. We tend to do this to ourselves because working in struggle and crisis is intense (and can give us a kind of high), but it doesn't have to be that way. In fact, we can choose to see things entirely differently. But making that choice, changing the way we think, can be really challenging.

Changing thinking styles from struggle-focused to ease-focused is like going from driving to flying.

I don't have a pilot's license.

But when people fly planes, they need an extra dimension of control—literally. Unlike cars, planes can go up and down as well as forward, back, right, and left. So the stick (or the yoke, depending on your plane) pulls back and pushes forward, in addition to steering.

Pushing forward takes you down, pulling back takes you up.

Simple.

But.

If you're used to driving a car, it must take some time to remember that there are more options. You've probably spent most of your life watching people drive cars. You kind of know how they work before you ever sit behind the wheel, if you ever do. But planes are usually a different story. It takes time to remember.

Pull back to rise.

And also.

It's not intuitive.

We tend to lean forward to go faster; we tend to think that the more intense we get, the higher we go.

Not always true.

Even when it is true, it might not be the best way to *make* it true.

As intensives, we specialize in those moments when we are speeding toward the ground, lights flashing, smoke rising, and then we decide to do this crazy thing so we make the dive even steeper and then in the five seconds before we crash we pull off this fancy spin and get lift and shoot skyward.

We get so used to doing that—and being asked to do that—that we sometimes forget it's not the only way to create lift. That under ordinary circumstances, lift is barely a thing. You just pull back on the throttle and gently, easily, up you go.

No smoke, no flashing lights, no barrel rolls.

No adrenaline.

Unfortunately, stress and depression are sort of addictive. If you experience them enough, your brain ends up with more receptors for the stress hormones than for the happy ones, and this can actually make you *create* stress for yourself if you aren't getting enough of to keep those receptors busy. (Janette Dalgliesh, a marvelous coach out of Australia, has some fascinating work on this subject.) The bad news is, you can end up "sabotaging" yourself and not get the outcome you were planning on because those receptors want their fix. The good news is, you can correct it by spending so much time happy and relaxed that the balance of available receptors shifts to prefer happy and relaxed brain chemistry.

So back to our airplane. Except when you're in crisis, there's more than one way to rise—and there are options that don't include nosedives. So if you catch yourself thinking, "Okay, time to go up to cruising altitude, guess I'd better get ready to dive" and putting on a crash helmet and a five-point harness, think again.

Let's think about this scenario:

You've started a business. You quit your day job. The business isn't a disaster, but it's not meeting your financial needs yet. What can you do?

- You could give up and go back to your job.

- You could insist that it's going to work no matter what and get into a serious financial crisis.

- You could consider a side gig to help fund it.

- You could borrow some money to tide you over.

- You could hustle your ass off and compromise a little to stay "in the field" while you get established.

Any of these would be possible. But some of them will be more stressful than others. Some will be more possible than others. Depending on your situation, some may not be possible at all. But think about it before you reject solutions.

You may find, somewhere in the depths of your brain, that you think the easy solutions, whatever they are for you, "don't count."

Privileging the struggle is an incredibly common thing among intensives, and *we have to stop because it's killing us*. Of course, it's not just us. But we are leading the charge. We are the ones saying it's only a real mountain climb if you go up the steep trail, that thank you for the compliment but the lifelong virtuoso has set a much better standard, that next time we're going to go all Martha and raise the cows for the milk for the compound butter.

No.

People, no.

This is absurd.

Compound butter still tastes good when it's made with butter you did not make yourself from those cows in the backyard. Take the compliment and run with it.

Say thank you. Mean it. Someone is impressed with what you did, not with what you didn't do. Stop focusing on your flaws and could-have-beens. You're an intensive and you did something awesome. Period.

Awesomeness is objective. It's not based on whether there was a harder way to do it. Just go ahead and accept that the thing, exactly as executed, was awesome. And *you did it*.

When you reject a compliment with a "could have done it harder," you are often unwittingly telling the person in question that their aspirations aren't even worth your acknowledgment. This dismissal effect is especially relevant if you're speaking with an expansive. They are admiring it—and you're saying it wasn't good enough. They might not even be able to do what you did. Be careful. The people who admire you are some of your greatest supporters, and they have better perspective than you do. You're right in the middle of your thing. They're the ones with distance.

You are an intensive; you will, by nature, surround yourself with people who are at or above your level of expertise and experience. Those are the people you seek and those are the people who inspire you and drive you forward. So when you compare yourself to your community, that's not the same as comparing yourself to the population at large. Things that come easily to you *and to everyone you know* might still be really extraordinary. You are probably swimming in a sea of intensives and experts, unless you have deliberately avoided it.

Everyone around me, for example, seems to be a coach or a sex educator. The stuff I talk about isn't a big deal to any of my peers. Talking about sex in the first place is just no big deal. Similarly, being a good, responsive lover who draws my lovers into sexual depth is kind of normal. But when someone is impressed or delighted, I need to remember that my pond is full of very special fish and that not everyone thinks this stuff is normal. It may be true that I could do better, but it is also true that what I do is pretty damn good.

All by itself.

It doesn't need comparisons to find its place.

And neither do you.

You do not need comparisons to know how good you are. You're good all by yourself.

PART TWO

OTHER PEOPLE

2 – 1

INTEGRITY

The flip side of "It doesn't have to be hard" is "integrity makes it easier in the long run."

This means that ease is not always found in the easy way out.

When it comes to integrity, in typical intensive style, either we value it or we don't. Typically there's no middle ground. Intensives who don't value integrity—and there are plenty—become very good at jobs that involve convincing the public of something, like doing PR for tobacco companies. People like that make me extra uncomfortable, because I value integrity very highly indeed.

However that doesn't mean that those of us who do value integrity are off the hook and patrons of virtue. Not. At. All.

In fact, our slippery little brains can set off to justify everything that we want to do, because we truly do feel out of alignment if we think we're out of integrity—and the Internet provides so much "research" that almost anything can be justified.

We have to watch out for this. Because if we don't watch out, we can end up *wayyyyyy* out of integrity with no way to put the toothpaste back in the tube, which can make us feel like crap, which can send us into depression or addiction or some other really unpleasant wormhole.

No thank you.

Here's an example. Say you're a lawyer, and you really like your intern. They're awesome. They're smart and interesting and talented and they're going to make a great lawyer. You enjoy the work, and you enjoy mentoring them.

So far, so good.

You develop, after a while, a kind of crush.

Now, you know that interns and the people they work for have a clear power imbalance that cannot be corrected for. Furthermore, you're quite a bit older. And they have a sweetheart already.

But they are cute and attractive and you're spending a lot of time together.

Your brain starts making up excuses, legit-sounding ones, about why you have to work late together. You take lunches to discuss cases. You stop by their desk to give them pointers.

You are, absolutely, within the letter of the law.

But you already know, somewhere in your intuition, that this is not *actually* why you're spending all that extra time with them. You *know* you've got a crush. You've already bopped yourself on the head with a rolled newspaper about it. You are on slippery ground.

If you keep justifying, you will cause yourself major trouble. (Or you very well could.) Also, you will be out of integrity. At a minimum, *you* will feel icky.

If you stop, you will feel pouty and like you want a cookie.

So now what?

You need community. Friends are not just a nice-to-have, they're the checks and balances in your internal governance. Because intensives have a tendency to go haring off on one wild idea or another, we need our people. So you have friends. You need them. And sometimes, especially when your inner alarm bells are ringing, you even need to listen to them.

We're talking really close, honest friends here, friends who can say, "Go you!" and make you dinner after they've heard the thing that most scares you. Because if you cut off your awareness of desire and pleasure, you're losing one of the very best tools you've got. But if you feel desire and pleasure, then you're likely to want very much to indulge them. You need a community to support you when you make right-but-hard choices. There's no judgment and no condemnation. *Yes* the intern is attractive and *yes* it's fine to notice but *no* it's going to make you feel like shit if you do stuff you shouldn't, so *don't do it.*

Either you're going to stuff your feelings or you're going to need some support for getting it right.

When you get it wrong, you hurt people, and if you value integrity you're really, *really* going to hurt people and simultaneously lose respect for yourself.

Your sneaky brain will look for ways you can keep respecting yourself, which means throwing shade where it doesn't belong—on other people, for not policing your behavior.

Sorry, but no.

It is no one's responsibility but yours if you transgress your own ideals.

If you do this long enough, you will start acting like the people you most despise.

Yuck.

So. Rewind.

Step one: When you feel not-quite-right about something and you are spending a lot of time justifying it in your head, listen to the first feeling. Justification is one of your superpowers, and you're using it for evil. Put. It. Down. This includes when you stay in an abusive relationship and when you take advantage of your power position and when you get into an affair and when you decide you don't have to follow the rules at work. Just nope.

Step two: Get support. Find people who are not directly affected by the choice who also have integrity, and tell them you want a reward. The pleasure centers of your brain are jonesing. Feed them. You want approval and accolades. Get someone who loves you and indulges you (but is probably not your partner) to give you the applause you want. This will help to assuage the sulk.

Why this works: Your pleasure centers are alive and awake and that's awesome. They run your intuition. But when they think something would be awesome and you say no, you make them whiney. By giving them a substitute boost, you keep them happy and online. Once you start down the path of justification, you're in trouble.

Debrief: After the fact, you can dissect the situation to get useful information. What were you actually hoping to get or experience from the thing you had to say no to? Your inner motivation was probably for some primal thing. Security. Love. Being desired. Feeling strong. Use that information to find a better way to address that need.

Your innards are some of the best resources there are. And you have exclusive access to them. Use them!

A word about being led astray: Every so often your intuition will be *wrong*. *Super* wrong—because you're an intensive and go big or go home, right? You will be sure someone is Okay. They will not be. *All* the people around you will be either telling you out loud or telling you with their choices and behavior that the someone is Not Okay.

If everyone you trust is screaming about that cliff—or even quietly and rationally mentioning the cliff—then, even if *you* don't see the cliff, maybe you better get a hang glider just in case. Which is to say, *listen* to them. You have built a community of smart, intuitive people around you. (You have, right? Because if not, get started.) When they yell "FIRE!," you should pay attention even if you don't smell a thing. You may not choose the same solution they suggest (they probably think you need to leave the building, but you go get a hose) but you should assume that three or seven or fifteen of your trusted friends can't be wrong. And if you're in a situation where you're trying to justify a choice but you really can't tell what you're justifying, make a list of all the people who have warned you about it. Even a little bit. Your sneaky reward brain will have damped down their voices so you can barely hear them, even though they are speaking at normal volume. So, if you have to, make a list. And then decide if all those people are so much stupider than you that you can't possibly be wrong.

Then think about telling them that to their faces.

Then seriously reconsider your choice.

The people you gather around you are *your people*. If no one dissents, they're not listening. If one person dissents, you're probably on the right track. If everyone's shaking their heads, though, you *might* be wrong. I know it's hard to imagine, but it could happen.

This process could save your ass.

2 – 2
FALLING FOR FRIENDSHIP

Let's talk about intensives and friendships and love and sex!

This is the area in which we most often discover that we are intensive. Here's how it goes: We're seven. Or twelve. Or twenty-seven. We make a friend. We like the friend. We go through the process of getting to know them a bit.

And then we invite them to spend time with us almost incessantly.

When we connect with someone, we want to learn everything about them right away. So we spend as much time as possible with them. We ask them all the real and serious and interesting questions. We call them first thing or last thing. We do this for maybe a couple of weeks or a couple of months.

It doesn't go on forever.

We are laying groundwork.

Once the groundwork is laid, we know we can come back to it whenever we want.

Once we are sated, we back way off. Like everything else we do, we take a rest. And then we get together with our friends sometimes, when we want, kind of like everyone else does. But because we laid that groundwork, we are really deep into the friendship already. Now when I call you, I can talk to you about my deepest darkest secrets with no preamble, because we *know* each other.

Expansives take their time. They go for coffee. Two weeks later they have lunch. After six months or a year, they get to the deeper intimacy that the intensives got to in two weeks. It's not better or worse, just different. But when intensives and expansives try to make friends with each other, the intensives think the expansives don't like them and the expansives feel like the intensives are unhealthy, overwhelming, and obsessed. It's just two different paths to the same end. Intensives go up the cliff; expansives take the long route with all the switchbacks.

We intensives are fiercely loyal. Sometimes we form strong bonds, but sometimes we just dive in for six months and disappear again. Either one can happen and be totally real.

If we're seven, our parents put a stop to the all-the-time thing eventually, unless the friend lives next door.

If we're twelve, someone thinks we have a crush. (Oh no, honey, a crush is so much more than this...)

If we're twenty-seven, we've learned to keep it mostly to ourselves, probably. We see them a little and then wonder how much more we should see them. We overthink it and stay away and then they probably end up thinking that we didn't want to be friends anyway. Or something. It becomes very confusing.

It shouldn't be. When we like someone, we like them *a lot*. That's part of it. But a much bigger part is that we like to get to know people deeply *right away*. Just like we approach projects and new learning goals, we set out to be friends thoroughly.

We tend to hold everyone, past and present, in our hearts. Someone from six months ago? Someone from six years ago? Someone from sixteen years ago? Check, check, check. Generally those friendships aren't "over" even if it's been sixteen years. The people in question may or may not feel the same way. It can be odd and awkward when someone you see as an old friend treats you as barely an acquaintance. But it happens.

It happens *a lot*.

Now, it goes without saying that if you are making friends with another intensive, you will likely go through this phase together, drift apart by mutual unspoken agreement, and not feel weird at all about calling each other up a year later with deep and intimate details of something, having connected in the interim only via social media. It is likely that you will share resources that you feel are abundant in your life easily and freely. It is also likely that you will randomly send each other extravagant letters, gifts, whatever your currency of affection is—not because you're trying to be overbearing, but because it feels totally appropriate.

Your parents will disapprove, unless they are also intensives. You will ignore them, almost certainly. This is your standard for friendships. You figure if you're not there to stay up all night, buy expensive and unnecessary gifts, visit for three weeks to help with the new baby or the surgery, volunteer in their new business to help it get off the ground, give them a twice-weekly healing service that they couldn't possibly afford, hire them for something because they can't possibly afford to do anything if they don't get work... If that's not what friends are for, what's the point?

And you tend to receive such tokens in the same spirit.

If they think they are buying your affection, they are wrong. If they think you are attempting to buy their affection, they are wrong. This is what affection *looks* like.

Seriously.

Doesn't everyone do this?

Well, no. And that's why people seem so disillusioned with the state of friendships these days. All those passive-aggressive memes on the Internet about "You probably don't love me enough to do XYZ, let's see who does" are a terribly backhanded way to say, "I want some real connection to real people, please! I want to see people and love people and be with people! But I don't know how to ask and I know how to complain, so I'll use the only tool I have and hope someone hears me."

It's a terrible strategy. But it's all a lot of people seem to have.

When someone doesn't take our intense start and intense reengagement as sincere, we can be very hurt. We don't hold back when we get into friendships. We dive in. We give everything. We show the fuck up.

We are being real and honest about how we feel when we do this. Someone who gets offended or defensive is probably someone who has been hurt a lot, and also probably an expansive—or an intensive who got beaten down for this kind of thing so many times that they see it as problematic and deviant and unhealthy.

It's only unhealthy if you don't back off.

Because after a while, just like falling in love, you need to ease back. You need to see the rest of the world, too. You need to get back to your hobbies, your wild ideas, your job, and your three side gigs. You need a whole, three-dimensional life. You're used to obsessing about things, so you might not notice at first. In fact, tearing yourself away from the comfortable pattern of spending most of your time with one person might be really uncomfortable. But it's appropriate and totally fine, it's necessary, and typically it will lead to a spurt of creativity.

Our obsessive phases are like overlapping wave patterns. Intensives have a sort of sine wave: Interest goes up, interest goes down. Our sine waves overlap so that, as interest in one thing goes up, interest in something else goes down. And then, every so often, because the two waves are slightly imperfectly offset, they both go down at once. The depth often becomes additive, and we seem catatonic for a while. And then sometimes they overlap going up. This is not, however, how expansives work.

2 – 3
HOW TO BE FRIENDS
WITH AN EXPANSIVE

Sometimes you meet someone awesome. You have all kinds of things in common with them. You like them! They seem engaging and interesting and nice.

And you can tell you're teetering on the edge of "too much."

Be gentle—they don't deal with information dumps as well as you do.

But *tell them.* Tell them you're an intensive. Tell them what it means. Tell them what your patterns are, up front. (Not too much!) TMI and "oversharing" are concepts that, while useful for everyone, were pioneered by overwhelmed expansives who forgot they had sovereignty and a delete key. Just give them a sentence and let them ask questions. (If you aren't sure how to approach this, think of it as being like starting sex ed with a seven-year-old. You want to give them something to begin with, but you also want them to lead, ask questions, and decide when to stop.)

If they run screaming at this point, they are probably never going to be more than an acquaintance. *Or* they are a squished intensive and you will see them in a year, eager for more information.

If they stick around, ask them to help you by saying no when they have had too much—or, preferably, a little before that.

Honor that no. Seriously. Not even kidding. Expansives can be very sensitive, but it's the right thing to do anyway. When someone says "I can't hang out," don't take it personally—but also, don't push.

Really.

Don't surprise them by showing up. They will put up with you showing up until they get annoyed, pick a fight, and never talk with you again.

The parallel to this is deconditioning a fellow intensive. Intensives are inclined to directness, but we have been conditioned and trained over our lifetimes not to be direct. It may take a fellow intensive several tries before they realize that you *really mean it* when you ask them to say no if they mean no. You might have to practice with each other, saying no and not having the other person get mad. It takes time to learn that it's really okay. I've had this experience with both friends and lovers over the years, and it's really disorienting the first several dozen times (or months) that you get a direct response or that someone believes you. Expansives may well go more gently—kind of like Minnesotans—and you might even make someone uncomfortable with your directness before you're really clear.

On the other hand, if you're too direct with an expansive, they might find you abrasive, blunt, or rude.

An intensive will know (or assume) that you didn't mean to be abrasive—unless they've been trained too thoroughly by expansives. Ferreting out other intensives can take time. Give yourself that time.

2 – 4

FALLING IN LOVE

When we fall in love, as intensives, we want it all, right away, just like that. It works that way with friends, too,

In an interview with Andy Drish[1], Elizabeth DiAlto talks about how relationships can be focused on growth, pleasure, or stability, and how we tend to shift around between the three. *However:* If you're an intensive, you're probably mostly into growth and pleasure. Stability is where you go to rest, but you have to remind yourself to go there. If your partner is an expansive, you may find that they are into pleasure and stability, or even just stability.

Occasionally you sync up, usually when there's been a period of fierce growth for a while and you're exhausted. But if you are always at odds, take a look at that model and see if it has some useful framing for you.

Sometimes you fall in love with your friends, new or old. And sometimes you fall hard.

Sometimes it's okay to be easy—easy to meet, easy to get to know,

---

1   https://www.youtube.com/watch?v=ZMCOgGoAv3g

easygoing. We tend to keep high, high standards for the people we spend time with. We tend to hold people at arm's length until we've decided about them. That can be useful. But when you're building community, let people in. They can smell fake and distant a mile away, and one thing we don't do well is fake. Welcome people. Embrace their presence in your life. Let them be who they are; don't expect everyone to meet the same standard you do. Radical acceptance might be a good exercise—let people be exactly who they are and love them for it. They won't all be your bosom buddies, but they might be nice to know.

Falling in love is an intensive's dream activity. It's all-engrossing, feels good, and involves deep and meaningful connection to another person who wants deep and meaningful connection to you.

Courtship used to be a real Thing, back in the day. You flirted, you met up at the town contra dance, you walked up the lane and back together, you might even eventually hold hands. You sent each other letters. It took time, courtship did, in part because it could readily lead to marriage.

We don't tend to court anymore—we just grab coffee, do dinner and a movie, and then hit the sack, only to break up five weeks later.

Only you might not, because you're an intensive. You get to know someone down to their *toes* if you can. You spend days and nights together. You stay up late. You watch obscure art films or go to the museum of questionable medical devices. You send them texts and emails, you want to talk with them all the time, you find out what they like to eat and you cook them dinner, you find out what they like to read and you buy them every book by that author, one every week. You are an exquisite, over-the-top paramour. And if they are intensive, you might be perfect. If they are not, or if they've been burned once too often, then you might just flatten them under the steamroller of your advancing love.

This is not good.

(I'm going to use the singular a lot here, because almost always these interactions are with one person. This is not to imply that you might not have multiple partners in your life, just that any one conversation is likely to be with one individual.)

Overwhelming someone with love and affection and joy and love is much more likely to be a problem if you're more intensive than the person you're falling for. Another intensive might just come back as thick and rich and excited as you are.

Learning to back off and dial it down is very tricky, because you don't want to muffle your intensive self, but you don't want to ask them to marry you on the first date, either (unless you really, really do).

Step One: Only do half the things that occur to you.

Step Two: Follow the Keep It Simple rule. If you have an idea (hey, I could send them a flower!) and then it blossoms (I could send them a dozen roses every day for a week!), go back to plan A. Keep it simple (and cheap). Save the grand gestures for, say, the wedding.

If the idea of a wedding (or the idea of keeping it simple) makes you want to puke, that's good information, too. The flip side is that if they aren't being all over the top with you? That's not necessarily a bad sign. They might just have a little less intensiveness.

Part of this intense focus on the object of our affections can be that we drop everyone else and everything else like a hot potato.

I don't actually need to tell you this is a bad idea, do I?

It teeters precariously on the edge of codependency.

Don't do it. Even if you have to make a standing date with two friends and take a pottery class on Tuesdays, do whatever it takes to keep from going all the way down the rabbit hole with each other. Neglecting everything and everyone else in our lives is so tempting! After all, there's this amazing person who is really fantastic and worth so much love and energy and attention. Work can wait, friends can wait, projects of passion can wait, sometimes even pets can wait, unless they are super portable or super cute.

This isn't healthy. It's just not. When you feel yourself falling in love, call your five best friends. Tell them you're falling for someone. Give them strict instructions to bug you until you treat them with respect, return their phone calls, and even initiate hangout time after an initial grace period of six weeks to three months. Enlist your community (the one you put love and respect and caring into, the one with all the great honest people who tell you what's up for real) to tell you you're being an ass and that you need to hang out with other people. If your sweetheart can't understand that with a few gentle and loving conversations, you might have picked someone who's more possessive than is healthy.

Of course, when you're not dodging pitfalls, there are also incredible benefits.

As partners, intensives are:

- **Loyal, loyal, loyal.** Once we decide we love someone, we are *there*. Completely. Hell, high water, and a direct letter from the Almighty won't keep us from supporting someone we love. If you need us? We're there. Middle of the night in a driving rainstorm when you break down on the border of Wisconsin? We're there. Our partners get the benefit of the doubt (unless we're processing old trauma), the priority in our calendar, and a kind of deep, unshakeable love that's hard to describe, especially as we mature and begin to understand what unconditional love really is.

- **Fabulous lovers.** We love to make love, and we tend to be very good at it. We research it, we practice it, we dive into it. We are adventurous, we are (in the words of Dan Savage) good, giving, and game, and we are deeply interested in deep connection.

- **Invested in our relationship's and partner's success.** We love the people we love with all our hearts, and we want to see them flourish. We may find jealousy more readily, but when we are secure we are also better wired for *compersion*—for taking pleasure in our loved ones' pleasure. We want the relationship to succeed, and we will turn our considerable force to that; we also want our beloveds to succeed. The risk is that they will feel pushed; the benefit is that they will not lack for encouragement. Just make sure the encouragement is for what *they* want, not what *you* want for them.

At our best, we can also be:

- **Flexible.** Change of plans? No problem. Need us to hit the road for six months? Just as long as we don't have any commitments. We like the new, the novel, the possible, and the unlikely. As long as it doesn't mess with something we're already planning, it's fine.

- **Adventurous.** We are the people who order the thing we've never heard of on the foreign-language menu when we're traveling. We would rather take the road less traveled and we want to get moving badly enough to jump in first, even if we don't know what we're doing. Think Tris and Tobias from *Divergent*: we are fierce and strong and deal with stress by diving into it.

- **Open to growth and change**. We like to learn. We

like new things. We don't always like giving up what we already think is right, but we kick ass at picking up what works best for us.

When you give yourself over to love, that's the deepest, most profound, most life-changing surrender of all.

Like everything else, we don't fall in love by half-measures. We fall in love all the way or not at all. If you've never been in love, take a look at what you're controlling. Trying to control your love is possibly the most exhausting thing you can do. If you've had a rough history, you might have learned it as a coping skill, but really, you're going to hurt either way so you might as well get to feel good when you can.

We are the people who never stop loving the people we love.

We are the people who hang on by fingertips and teeth, who work our asses off to stay in a relationship. We are those people. We are fiercely loyal. We are unbelievably persistent.

And we are like that because when we are done, *we are done*.

We hate that feeling, so we try *really hard* not to let it happen.

Love is real and deep for us. We take it seriously, like everything else, but more so. Wounds and betrayals cut us deeply, and it's worth it to repair them wherever possible.

So we try like crazy.

But when we give up, that, too, is a surrender.

The surrender we resist most fiercely is external reality. We have learned that most of the time we can bend reality to our will, we can make it do what we want. We can, by being ourselves, change the story. So when we can't do that, it's disorienting and identity-shaking. Surrendering to the few things we can't change is terrifying, because as intensives we learn that we are magicians. If we can't change the world, who are we?

The answer, of course, is that mostly we *can* change the world, and when we can't, it's the exception that proves the rule; we can learn to roll with the immutable parts so we can save our energy for the stuff that we are compelled to transform. Surrender is a part of effective world-changing work.

And once we learn that, very little is actually out of reach.

If you believe at all in the Law of Attraction--the idea that you draw into your life experiences and things that you focus on, this is a useful set of concepts. You can't go around in a state of resistance. It just doesn't work. But by saying yes more often you can change what is available for change.

2 – 5
ACROSS THE LINE:
LOVING AN EXPANSIVE

What if you fall in love with an expansive? How do you do that?

When you're with an expansive partner, it's particularly important to follow the three rules: Keep yourself busy, see their gifts, and give them room to move and be themselves.

Do not try to convert them. Do not meet them in the middle. Make room for both of you to be who you are.

Concretely, that could look like this: Rather than hanging over their shoulder, set up a regular check-in time on any project you're working on (like planning a vacation, or a major holiday, or a renovation) together, maybe once a week. Other than that, no asking questions. If they volunteer information, that's a different story, but *no asking*. Pretend it's almost your birthday and you can't see the package behind the coat in the closet.

It could look like this: Have a gratitude journal where you write five things you appreciate about them every night.

It could look like this: Keep a running list of things you can do instead of fretting over how your partner is managing their part of the project. Do those things. Have a friend be an accountability buddy for doing those things and not fretting. Maybe even get an activity buddy.

It's important to hold your boundaries with yourself in this process. Make sure that you aren't overstepping your own lines. It's not about what your partner does, although you may well be used to managing other people. It's about what *you* do. What are you feeling? How can you change *your* behavior to ease any discomfort you might have? This is about responsibility. It's about ownership (of yourself and your shit). This is about doing *your* work on *your* feelings. When we get impatient we tend to think that if the other person would just do it our way, everything would be fine. This is, naturally, bullshit. But we get like that in our enthusiasm/power/ intensity. This is a chance to make a different choice. How many people have gotten fed up with you and your habit of thinking you're always right?

Sometimes that's people being expansive and you being clear and communicative. But sometimes you're actually *not right about everybody*.

You already know that people vary, because the world is mostly expansives, and here you are an intensive wondering why no one gets you. People vary. You're different. (People have probably told you that, too.) But *because* people vary, because people are different, because you, specifically, are different, what's right for you is unlikely to be right for someone else.

This, unfortunately, makes you actually wrong. Very wrong. And if you're trying to *make* the other person in your life behave in the way that would work for you, you're doubly wrong.

I'm sorry. I know you hate being wrong. And if they *were* you, you'd be right. But if they were you, they wouldn't be fighting you—unless they had a rebellious-against-authority habit. Not that you do, I'm sure, ever. But you hate being wrong. That's why you like to be the authority.

Guess what?

Hang up your expert hat. Let *them* be right about them. Even if you think they're wrong. If you're lucky, the you-always-right thing will just have been annoying. If you're not lucky or if you also have a violent streak, it's totally possible that this habit has created an unhealthy pattern where they just assume they have to go along with you, which has created in you the feeling that you're all alone, Taking All The Responsibility For Both Of You, Poor Thing.

Suck it up.

You created this monster because you couldn't tolerate anything else. Time to un-create it. Not by deciding that your partner sucks, but by actually stepping back and making room for them to lead and create and have authority in their way, not in yours. This means letting go of control and supporting them in decisions even when it's not the way you would have done it (and it won't be).

Unless someone is going to die as a result, just *let it be*. Occupy yourself. Lead yourself. Choose for yourself. Give some of the responsibility and control over to them. Because when you're a jerk about it, everybody loses. Instead, talk with them. Be transparent and honest. Make space. Back the fuck off.

It's good for you.

If your expansive partner seems like they are withdrawing a little, double-check with a friend. They might be breaking up with you, only you're too committed to hear it. Intensives take relationship commitments very seriously, and we don't tend to let go easily. We tend to figure that hard stuff is what gets worked through so we can get back to the good part. Expansives can be more easy come, easy go. They might be very dedicated, but it's equally possible that they aren't capable of being half as into you as you are into them, no matter how good it is—and they will let go that much more easily. You can try to hang on, but the odds are not in your favor. Much more likely (*much* more likely), they are drifting away.

If you don't want this particular lesson (hold your own shit, back off, and if they're going, let go) as your daily diet, and you're looking, *don't date an expansive. Date another intensive.*

2 – 6
LOVING AN INTENSIVE

I noticed a few years ago that most of the couples I knew from college were still together. I graduated in 1997. That's a long time ago. What's more, they were mostly still happy. My fellow alumni noticed, too. I finally narrowed it down to Something Funny In Admissions and at long last, pinpointed it: My alma mater mostly only admits intensives. The few expansives who are accepted usually leave after a year. It's an intensive environment. *Everyone* is doing fifty things for fun in their spare time and wishes they had enough time to double-major, but they don't because a single major is *so intense*. And when intensives get together with intensives they tend to be happy together and stick. Because we love it, and because we are stubborn.

If you date another intensive, it's easier…or at least different. It's not all cakewalk. Just some of it.

This can be a holy terror of a roller coaster, or a whole bucket of fun.

On the plus side: The sex is *hot,* as long as you stay connected.

Everything is interesting. If not, one of you is depressed.

You both love your own stuff. You both love to *see* each other love other stuff. You will spend time on your own stuff and time together, and the only problem will be *not enough time.*

Or space. The odds that you will need a ton of space for all your interests and hobbies are pretty high. On the other hand, you might decide to go on the road in a tiny house or hike the Appalachian Trail together. With your five-year-old kid. Because why not? One extreme or the other is much more likely than the suburban three-bedroom, 2.5 bath, slow-and-steady existence. You might have that house, but you'll be haring off to the woods every weekend to LARP or jetting off to London or working on your startup.

When you're in love, you're *so in love.* When you're mad, holy shit, watch out.

Pro tip 1: Do *not* let moments of anger determine what you do next. *Especially* do not break up over them.

This is an important and hard-won lesson.

Your anger is fierce and beautiful and huge.

It does not represent what will be true when the storm blows over.

You get to have your anger. In fact, the only way for it not to be toxic is for you to let it flow into and through you, and then out. You can't avoid it.

Your anger is not usually actually about the other person. It is about expectations missed, it is about disappointment, it is about wishes and hopes and dreams and bad communication, but the odds are good that it is as much about you not doing something you expect of yourself as it is about the other person's behavior. Either that or you trying to change someone other than yourself, which is outside your scope of practice. You only get to change yourself. However, by changing yourself, you may change others. Systems theory tells us that, because we are all interconnected, any change in a system tends to influence the whole rest of the system. That includes the other person. But changing *because you want to change someone else* is not a clean and direct move. Changing *because you want to be different* and enjoying the resulting changes in others—now that's great stuff.

In any case, your anger will come and feel urgent and fill your whole field of vision—and then it will go. You might hang onto the emotional backlash or the exhaustion or the pain for a while, but your anger, that urgent, blinding, fight/flight/freeze feeling, will pass on, and what is left behind will be very different. Do not make any major decisions. Do not say words that cannot be unsaid. Do not set up patterns that will become extra entrenched because they began in this highly emotional and negatively charged context.

Do let yourself be angry.

Go outside. Shout at the ocean or the trees or the sky. Burn the energy with physical activity. Keep reminding yourself that this will pass and that you'll have something different to say and think in just a little while.

Do not, do not, *do not* make major decisions or end relationships in this state. Don't. Just don't. It will wear out your relationship over time, like bending a piece of steel back and forth until it snaps.

Pro tip 2: Get a therapist. Meet quarterly unless there's a crisis, in which case, meet weekly. This will keep you and the therapist ready and aware and nimble.

You will have so many ideas. You will have to pick. You will hate having to pick. That won't change that you have to pick.

You will be more likely than your average person to be monogamish or polyamorous (see the sidebar for a little more on these terms). *Or* you will be very jealous. Or both. It *is* possible to reduce the impact of jealousy on your life, if you would otherwise like to explore less conventional relationship structures. You have a lot of love, and probably a lot of sex drive. You will want to see what happens when new opportunities present themselves. You will want to take (safe-ish) risks. And you will connect deeply and powerfully with a lot of people.

You will take more risks than you would in another kind of relationship.

You will probably also have more fun. (At least, it'll be fun for you. Others may differ.)

If you have kids, you will have to be extra sensitive if they are not intensives.

You will have unlikely groups of friends.

Definitions

monogamish: mostly monogamous with some exceptions, agreed upon by you and your partner.

polyamorous: having more than one, or the acknowledged potential for more than one, consenting and aware partner/lover at once. This can take many forms, but the idea is that you can have more than one sexual or romantic partner, all people can know this is happening, and everyone has said it's okay.

You will probably eat *very well* or neither of you will care.

Sensual pleasure or intellectual pursuits (or both) a will probably be central to your joy.

You will be *very good* at what you do: hobby or job or both. You will need to work to keep a balance between that and the person or people you love, or else you could just topple over into working all the time.

If you break up, it will probably be epic. Horrible and epic. (Not recommended.)

You are, however, intensives, so you are less likely than usual to break up. Intensives are fucking persistent. Also, we know how bad breakups can be.

You may be accused of being saccharine-sweet, but never boring.

If you partner with an intensive, it will be that much harder for you to connect with expansives, because you won't have the experience of accommodating them in your primary relationship. Expansives will continue to require more attention and work and they will sometimes be puzzling. However, some of your best friends will be expansives, and it will be a total relief to relax for a while around them—you won't realize how much energy you're always putting out to keep up with your partner.

Pro tip 3: You and your partner can go away to somewhere delightful and get a bit of a break if you try. But you *will* have to try.

If there is political or activist work in your world(s), you will be *very* into it. Watch out for arrest records. That joke about bailing out your best friend will not be a joke. But you'll feel great about it.

If your values diverge, you may have trouble. You will grow in many directions, including, sometimes, apart. This is why you need your therapist: Your underlying love can help you bridge this gap, but you have to do it on purpose sometimes.

You will need to support your partner even in most of their wild, crazy ideas. If they can't have wild, crazy ideas they will stop being themselves. But you can support them exploring the viability, too.

Pro tip 4: Don't get emotionally attached to your partner's projects unless you own them equally.

When you are attached to your partner's project, it becomes hard for you to let them do it their way.—and they're an intensive, so they *need* to do it their way. Doing it your way will just annoy both of you. They won't get it *exactly right* and they will be frustrated from trying to work in your brain instead of theirs.

Make sure there's space for *coming back together* at the end of whatever thing you've done. If you're in an open relationship, this includes after one of you has been with another love. But it also means after other things, like intense gaming sessions or spending a week deep in your personal project or launching a Thing at work. Make the space and time to really connect and be together, because if you don't, you can lose one another. The love stays, but everything else dissolves, including your ability to be intimate. We are stubborn, we are magic, but we can't prevent that dissolution except by good old-fashioned touch and speech and eye contact. Let your romantic side out. Invite it in your partner. Life will be so much better.

Here are your relationship keywords: love, joy, respect, possibility, YES!

2 – 7
INTENSIVES IN FAMILIES

Once upon a time, there was an intensive, and she lived in the best family EVER.

She got lots of sleep and ate exactly what she wanted, and no one minded.

She worked hard on projects, sometimes forgetting to eat right or sleep much. Her office fridge was stocked with the best foods for her to eat so she didn't have to think about it. When she was in the middle of a project, no one bothered her for anything else. Sometimes she was kind of short with people by accident, but no one took it personally.

While she was working on a project, her loved ones did whatever they wanted and kept living their lives. No one else stopped what they were doing because of her work.

But when she was done with a project, everyone took a break and celebrated with her, unless *they* were in the middle of a project. There were enough people around that *someone* could always celebrate. She loved her work, and she loved the high she got from getting through a major push.

She also loved to rest and recuperate. When she finished a project, her family would make sure to spend some extra time with her before she dived into something else. They would do special things together and really enjoy each other. No one thought it was strange that she would watch movie after movie or read a stack of novels before beginning again.

When she wanted to surprise someone with something special, she would work for days or weeks or months on it. Sometimes she'd do it all by herself and sometimes everyone except the recipient would be involved. People delighted in her beneficent mischief.

She loved sex and got lots of it.

She took her hobbies to extremes, but it was somehow important for her to do that. The hobbies fed the work; they helped her brain function better.

She bonded as much with her dog as with her kids.

She got excited a lot. Sometimes she forgot and made too much noise in a quiet place like a library or a fancy restaurant, but someone would just gently remind her. They also spent a lot of time in big places where big voices were welcome.

She went off on adventures suddenly, but no one took that personally, either. And she always came home full of ideas and energy.

Well…almost always.

When you were growing up, you probably got told to be quiet, settle down, and mind your manners, either at school or at home. And it probably felt like torture. Your family either consisted of other intensives, who understood who you would eventually be but felt that only adults should act like that, or of expansives who felt like no one should ever act like that and please, God, when were you going to grow out of it?

If you were lucky, you got neither of these but instead a family that nourished and cherished exactly who you were.

But even if you're lucky, there will be times when you are interacting with people whose lives affect yours, whom you may love very much (or not) but who absolutely do not get you because they are expansive. They probably wish you'd be more regulated: either up or down, either always energetic and enthusiastic or always calm, cool, and collected. They may cringe when you get excited about something in public or take it very personally when you keep working on your new project rather than coming to eat the delicious dinner they just made.

They love you, but they wish you'd change how you act, because it's making them either nervous or embarrassed or both. They may drive you up a wall with their "normal" attempts at interaction.

Sarah Grey, the editor of this book, tells this story about her own child: Our six-year-old intensive kid got a door hanger with a little dry-erase message board as her prize for selling Girl Scout cookies, and it's suddenly become a surprisingly useful tool. For instance: Sometimes in the morning I go in to wake her up and she's happy to see me; other times she starts screaming at me to get out. She's decided that now she can use her message board to tell me what she wants: "DON'T COME IN SAY IT IS 5 MINITS" was the message today (i.e., she wants a five-minute warning from outside the door). She also used it to say sorry yesterday after a tantrum. It's a way of having some control over her space, plus she's discovering that sometimes it's easier to say things in writing than out loud.

Now, the best solution would be for them to practice loving detachment, where who you are is *your* business and who they are is *their* business. But not only do people rarely work that way, *communities* rarely work that way. What that means is that even if both you and they come to an understanding that your behavior only reflects on you and they should carry on regardless, the principal of the school, their boss, and the restaurant manager will see things differently. You are perceived as a unit and so it *does* matter what you do. *What you do affects them.*

Not fair. But true.

There's an important caveat here: Sometimes you *are* just being inconsiderate, and intensiveness is not an excuse. Being clear about your needs and expectations can go a long way toward mitigating the tendency you have to get absorbed in 7our own projects. "Rude" is often code for "not acting expansive," but it can also be code for "you are acting like no one but you matters." If you are intensive, these are both possible.

How to resolve this? You may not care what people think of you. (Or you might! Being an intensive doesn't mean you're impervious to criticism. In fact, a lot of us are extra sensitive.) In either case, your family members care, because it affects them. And you love them, so you care that it affects them.

How does it affect them?

Expansives have a hard time with intensives, especially over long periods of contact. Expansives tend to take their time to make decisions slowly, with lots of data, which we only do when we really don't want to do something. They tend to wait and see. They tend to consider their options.

They tend to make us stark raving mad. We tend to make them so anxious they freeze. It sucks for all of us.

Fortunately, there's a solution: You can, to some extent, keep yourself busy while they do their thing. You can also talk about it directly.

How to stay busy until they're ready:

If you're an intensive, find something to obsess over while they make their pro/con lists or graphs or whatever it takes. You already know the answer; they don't. Go do something else and let them find their way there. You climbed the cliff; they're taking the scenic hike up the back of the mountain. They'll get there. Meanwhile, you get to stargaze. Remember that your cycle requires deep rest, too. Do that while they think. They're not going to even be winded when they get there, so you better be ready to keep moving.

They can pick something for you to obsess over and assign it to you. They can also tell you not to tell them the answer until they find it. And you can each be willing to hear the other one out if you come to different conclusions by your respective processes. I know this sounds like basic communication, but when it comes to making decisions, we tend to get very, very attached to our ideas.

Another way to improve your flexibility is to bring rough drafts instead of final editions to the table. Start the conversation while it's still unformed, so you're more open to input. Fall in love with the possibilities—all of them—so when you get to a conclusion it's not a disappointment.

If your kids are expansives, let them be expansives. Create space for them to have their process. Be prepared to answer question after question while they work through things. And if they need lots of lead time, plan for that. *You* might like spontaneity, but they might not. Or you might be willing to keep going and going in search of something; they might not. You've got an advantage over expansive parents with intensive kids—you've got the opportunity to keep ahead of them, easily. If your roles were reversed (as it may have been when you were a kid) the expansive parent spends a lot of time and energy running after the intensive kid, when what they need is space and time to think things through.

If you're an intensive and you have expansive friends whose kids are intensives, offer to take the kid for an afternoon. The kid will feel understood and the parent will get to breathe. If your kids are expansive, see if you can do a trade.

If your in-laws or cousins are expansives, love them for it. Let them do the fiddly parts of the planning if that's their talent. If they're the laid-back, anything-goes kind of expansive, then just know there are things that you will complete while they are still thinking about it. That's okay, as long as you all acknowledge it. See if you can have a direct conversation about your respective styles (joking about it is sometimes a great way to introduce it—but make fun of yourself, not anyone else) so you can actually talk about what works and what doesn't. If there's a simple task (go buy a garden hose) you can be done with it and on to the next thing, because you see that the opportunity cost of getting the wrong hose is negligible. On the other hand, a complicated task like buying a summer cottage will hit your obsession button, and you might need a more expansive person to help you stay rational when necessary. Play to your strengths and let them play to theirs. You can all benefit.

Sometimes that works. Sometimes it doesn't. Sometimes you just have to *tell* someone something and there's no easy way to make that happen.

You know their style is not yours. You're an intensive, they're an expansive, and the topic is volatile and loaded.

If they can handle direct communication, this will be easier. But that's a big if.

Here's a tiny detour into intercultural competency:

In the ICS inventory developed by Dr. Mitchell Hammer (http://www.icsinventory.com/) he describes two dimensions across which we communicate: we are either external or internal (loud and animated or quiet and restrained) and either prioritize ourselves or prioritize the group. This gives four possible quadrants: loud/self-oriented, loud/group-oriented, quiet/self-oriented, quiet/group-oriented.

Intensives are probably more common in some of these quadrants than others, and our upbringing has a lot to do with how we handle social situations and communication, but what's important is that if you're going to be clear and honest with someone, you take into account the match or mix of your communication styles. If you are loud and group-oriented (think the stereotypical Italian, fight big, make up big) and you're communicating with someone who is quiet and group-oriented (think the stereotypical Japanese: disagree subtly) then at least you have the group orientation in common. In both cases you're likely to agree that the needs of the group matter more than the needs of the individual, and that's a place to find common ground. But if you're loud, you might need a way to be yourself (not mute yourself) while simultaneously meeting their need for relative quiet and order in interactions.

How do you do that? Might be by creating space or distance: maybe you send an email or text, or set a date to talk on the phone. Might be by giving them a bit of a heads up that you're feeling energetic about something. Or it might be that there's an emotional space where you can meet one another and both feel safe—sometimes time-outside-of-time, trips, couples retreats, etc make it possible.

Now imagine that those differences, usually marked as intercultural, turn out to also apply (to some extent) to intensives and expansives. You might both be from the same family, but if one of you is group-loud and one of you is individual-quiet, you've got some bridge building to do.

2 – 8
HOW TO BE WRONG

Being able to be wrong goes a long way toward healthy family relationships, and it's one of the hardest things for us to do.

Being in disagreement about something and letting it happen anyway is the second most important and second-hardest thing for intensives to do. Often, you start to lose respect for the people in your family when they don't do things your way, especially if you've explained it to them. It's easy to believe that if they don't agree with you, you simply haven't explained it right, because if they understood you they'd obviously agree with you, because you're always right…

Right?

If you can't tell if you're doing this to your loved ones—if you're disrespecting them by accident—take a look at how you talk about your stuff.

How you relate to your possessions says a lot about how you relate to your loved ones.

To begin with, if we care, as intensives we want the best. We want the best so much that we tend to go overboard. We tend to upsell ourselves. We tend to buy the top-end, the best-reviewed, the premium version…if we care at all. If we don't care, we'll get whatever. But when we do care, watch out, because we will spend three times as much as we intended to in order to get the thing that works best. Also, we will often replace things that have the wrong feeling or energy even if they still work. This will drive everyone around us nuts; the best solution is to make enough money that no one else worries about what you're spending, or to be completely solo. If you have something you associate with a past relationship that went sour, you will remember that. The best thing is to start over from scratch with a new thing that has no association. This goes for tableware, appliances, everything—even if it's "perfectly good."

And you, as an intensive, will want to be in charge.

You'll want to own it, to have your name on the lease. If it's yours, it's YOURS. This is normal. You think you know the right way for things to be, and the best way to make sure that's how it happens is to be the owner. You don't mind taking responsibility for it, if that means control.

But needing to be in control of everything has two major drawbacks. Number one, it means you have a lot to pay attention to. Failing to share responsibility means that your brain and heart have to hold it all. The other drawback is that you're not connecting with or trusting anyone else. Put down the control freakout and back away slowly. Sometimes control is good strategy, but sometimes it's not. You will probably need some external perspective to figure that out. Ask yourself these things:

- What is the worst case if someone else is in control of this thing?

- What is the worst case if I'm in control of this thing?

- What is comforting to me about being in control?

- Do I have the resources to be in control/owning this thing?

- Is this where I want to put my resources right now?

It will become really clear, really fast, whether this is a thing you're doing because your ego is having a fit or because it's really a core value for you to be in control of this aspect of your life. It's also worth considering the impact that maintaining solo control of key things will have on your relationships, romantic, familial, and so on. It will be almost impossible to have an equal partner if you don't have an equal stake in your shared living space. It will also be almost impossible for you to be vulnerable in the same ways if you can always kick them out because it's not their space. Same with transportation and other factors.

If you are the one controlling it, you're setting up a power dynamic. That's fine if you're mostly relating to your kid or to people you're not in close relationships with, but the minute you become the one with the power, you need to think very hard about the impact you're having on the people around you. There's responsibility that you might like to blow off, but you can't do that. We intensives tend to step naturally into positions of control and power—for better and for worse. Unless you and your partner have an explicit agreement in which you have more power, and you've both chosen that, it can be very destabilizing for one partner to have that much more power than the other. It also, despite being natural, can be exhausting. It takes a lot of resources to track the thing(s) you're in charge of. Is that a choice you want to make? If so, make it a deliberate one. It's worth the extra time and energy to negotiate, both with your partner and more importantly with *yourself,* about what kinds of stressors or pressures you're taking on. If you take them on freely, that's a very different experience from waking up one day and discovering that you've taken on responsibility for a fully functional adult's housing or transportation by trying to control it.

How do you know what you believe, what matters, and what's getting in your way?

You work on your shit.

You ask yourself the hard questions, or you hire someone to help you out.

Why did you do that? Was it necessary? Was it unkind? What really matters to you?

Working on your internal stuff will give you the ability to choose vulnerability more easily. The vulnerability from shared property and responsibility and shared emotion and shared risk, and that sharing will lead to greater intimacy in the relationship in general.

What *we* have is *ours* is a good test phrase. If you talk about *my* house instead of *our* house, or *my* project or *my* remodel or *my* plan for next year, pay attention. You're probably exhausting yourself unnecessarily by taking on too much—and infantilizing your partner at the same time.

This is especially likely if your partner is an expansive.

Step back. Make some space. Hold some trust. And if you need to, have some serious conversations about what you're seeing and what patterns confuse you. Watch out for judgment, too—being deeply judgmental is another one of our not-so-pretty traits that can drive a wedge between us and the people we love.

1. What if you knew they were an adult who would handle whatever it was just fine, even if it wasn't the way you'd handle it?

2. What if you assumed that if they did something it was for a good reason?

3. What if you figured they probably had a perfectly

good idea?

These things can totally change the way you function in the world, leaving you with a lot more energy and both of you with a lot more trust and connection than you began with. It's really helpful, for sustainability, to check yourself and try to keep from being supercilious as much as you possibly can. You might be right. You might be wrong. Learn to ask yourself if it really matters this time, in this place, or if you can just let it go.

This especially goes for things like dirty socks on the floor. Does it bother you? Pick them up and put them in the hamper. That takes so much less energy than fighting about it, and it's a gesture of love. Try saying "I love you" every time you do it and see how it changes your view of socks.

If you are resentful, you are not respecting your partner.

Either you need to leave or you need to change your attitude, and then possibly request a change if you still think it's necessary. You cannot even negotiate from a place of disrespect.

So you've figured out how to have the conversation. How do you get started?

1. Start by telling them what you want to talk about. If they're not loud/direct, see if you can find the gentlest possible way to do that. You might even test your phrasing on a neutral friend first.

2. say you know that it's hard for them. Having their feelings acknowledged can change their whole experience. This is someone you love, or at minimum don't want to piss off. See how far across the bridge you can walk toward them.

3. invite them to talk about their experience and really LISTEN. Just listen. Pretend they're telling you a fairy

tale about some knight who lives in a castle in deepest darkest FarAwayLand. Be curious and interested.

4. invite them to troubleshoot with you, to find a way that you can handle it. Ask what would help them. Get on the same side of the negotiating table as they are.

5. express what's important to you in the situation, so that you don't end up feeling muted. Make sure you can say what you need.

6. find a place where you can agree.

So easy. So hard. So SO worth it. You're not too much. The goal of this conversation isn't, "How quiet should I be and where should I stand in the corner?"

The goal is, "I need to be loud and exuberant to express myself (or whatever is true for you.) How can I do that in a way that feels respectful of you and your relationships in our shared community? Let's find a way."

2–9
EVERY NORMAL
IS DIFFERENT

Assuming that you're not "normal" in your family context, if that's what's necessary, can be a little bit heartbreaking. But assuming that *everyone* has a different normal works a little bit better. So instead of saying "the world is mostly normal and then *over here there's me!*", it helps to say, "the world is full of all kinds of people and *this is my kind.*" While it may be true that the dominant culture is expansive, there are a lot of intensives out here! It's like M&Ms. We know green ones are rare, but they still exist. Know you're a green M&M—and go find the other green ones.

The Five Love Languages by Gary Chapman is a fantastic resource for normalizing all kinds of giving and receiving. It develops a model in which each of us receives love best in one or two of the following five ways:

(1) gifts;

(2) words of affection;

(3) shared time and activities;

(4) touch; and

(5) acts of service.

Concretely, this means that I might feel loved when you wash the dishes, walk the dog, and pick up my transit pass and you might feel loved when I spend the evening playing Scrabble with you. We usually tend to express love the same way we receive it best, so that means that you would get us concert tickets to say "I love you" and I would do the laundry. Only, if we're speaking our own languages, we might not hear each other, wouldn't "feel loved," and end up disconnected, even though we're both putting energy and attention into the relationship.

The idea that there are lots of "right ways" and approaches to life is gradually emerging everywhere. We also see it in the ideas of multiple learning styles (visual, auditory, kinesthetic-tactile), multiple family styles (polyamory, monogamy, coparenting, single), and multiple affectional, romantic, and sexual orientations (gay or lesbian, bisexual, queer, pansexual, aromantic, asexual), among others. Since postmodern thinking took root, there has been a shift in Western society from a belief in One Right Way to an understanding that many voices and ways are equally valid and that people vary. The 1950s fantasy of a monolithic cultural norm has been eroded to the point of no return. It was always an illusion. Identity is and has always been multiple and beautiful. It's the way people are. We have always been diverse. And when we get our heads out of our collective asses, intensives have always known this, really. We forget, in our intense-work-cave places, but when we emerge and think about it for a minute, we *expect* people to be different. And while it can frustrate us, it can also invigorate us. We thrive on difference and novelty.

As an intensive, you can watch the people around you to find out what they like and how they operate. Or you can just *ask them*. Finding out how to communicate your love so they can receive it is a great first step.

And then?

And *then* you get to do it. As an intensive you might *love* over-the-top extravagance. Others around you might prefer a slow trickle feed of tiny delights all year. You can be *amazingly awesome* at whatever it is that you're doing because they love it, even if it's not a thing you'd choose for yourself, even if it is fundamentally expansive—even if what your loved one needs is a nice, consistent sprinkling of love throughout everything, rather than the intermittent geyser blast that might come more naturally to you.

Again, take your intensiveness and step back, rather than dialing it down. Create space that makes it accessible to the less intensive people in your life. Remember, there is *nothing wrong with you* or your excitement and enthusiasm. You don't need to dial it down—really, you can't. *What you need to do is find the right place for yourself.*

As youth and as adults, we need to pay attention to ourselves and our contexts and make sure we are well-trained in the ways of love. I know that sounds like some kind of weird hippie advice from the sixties, but I could not be more up to date or more serious. The tools we have are the tools we will use. If we have a variety of methods for giving and receiving love and if we know how to see our challenges before they destroy us, that will go a long way toward protecting everyone.

Intensive children benefit from this at an early age—it's not something you want to put off until adulthood. When you teach us how to love well and often, we will use it to help the world. In fact, any tool is like that: If you give us love, or sex, or animal rescue, or hard work, or hiking, or dance—it doesn't matter what you put in our hands, we will use it to try to change the world. Our ability to see what we can do, and to understand that we hold a lot of power for good or evil, is vital. We don't think of ourselves as unusually strong, but we are. We can bull-in-a-china-shop our way through life if we don't know our size or power. And our frustration, anger, and fear are also outsized. By teaching us that we have great power and great responsibility—not to squish ourselves, but to avoid the china shop if needed, to redirect our passion, to choose contexts that work for us—we can be so much happier.

It's one thing to be an intensive. You know what's going on with *you*.

It's another thing to be in a company or a family with adult intensives. Even if they don't know they're intensives, they can reasonably be expected to be somewhat self-aware and act with a modicum of adult social skills.

But when your *kid* is an intensive, that's another whole story.

Having an intensive kid when you're not expecting one is a little like having a bomb go off in the middle of your perfectly normal life.

I say that entirely without rancor—I was a classic intensive kid. But if you were expecting "normal" (expansive) and got an intensive, you were probably blindsided.

As infants, intensive kids are often (but not always) what Dr. Sears calls "high needs children." These babies tend to:

- Need almost constant physical contact with one caregiver, usually the mother.

- Be unable to "settle" or "cry it out"—they will scream as long as needed to get contact and attention.

- Cosleep, often until age seven or older.

- Breastfeed, often past toddlerhood, just for the contact and comfort.

- Want more attention and more engagement than other children.

- Be fussy about things like texture or flavor or sleeping.

As they age, these kids:

- Worry about big ideas from a very young age, and do so with sophistication and depth.

- Crave autonomy and self-determination.

- Fight authority.

- *Hate* being condescended to or treated "like a kid."

- Are really smart.

- Require explanations for everything.

- Often act out in school.

- Are often not well served by traditional school structures.

- Need more physical activity than their peers.

- Engage with subjects that they like and are perfectly willing to fail ones they don't see a need for.

- Will not wear their coats when it's cold.

- Want things to be their idea.

- Say the darndest (and smartest) things.

- Sound like they're four going on forty.

- Often throw epic tantrums when they don't get what they want—but they're not being spoiled brats.

On that last point: when these kids act out, scream, yell, and throw tantrums, it's because they think their survival is at stake. When you insist on doing it your way with no explanation, the intensive kid's brain panics, believes that you don't see them, and concocts the same chemicals it would if they were about to be eliminated by a tiger. Their being, their existence in the world, is tied to having you recognize who they are and what they have to say.

There's really no way to avoid that panic reaction, except to hear them out, use reflective listening, and basically treat them like a tiny adult.

That's the key to intensive kids: Treat them like tiny adults with underdeveloped emotional management skills. Assume that their desires, ideas, worries, thoughts, joys, and fears are just as real and just as important as yours are. *Do not blow them off. Do not condescend to them. Do not make false threats or empty promises.*

Touch them a lot. Tell them you love them a lot. Build trust—which you have to earn, bit by bit. Earn their respect while you're at it. Assume they do understand and give them the information they need to make a healthy choice.

As for teaching them those emotional management skills: Model them yourself. Hold yourself to the same standards you hold them to, and explain how you handle it. Let them be exuberant whenever you can. And when they are struggling, give them grownup-sized emotional management tactics, because their emotions are *huge*, much bigger than their little bodies. Acknowledge how scared they might be, and how frustrated. Give them language. Give them every tool in your toolkit. Show them how to be intensively authentic without hurting anyone. Examine your judgments about what is "appropriate" and what is not. If their chosen response is actually just fine, make room for them to do it. Society has spent years training you to have expansive expectations for yourself and your kids alike. Reject the old model and make room for them to be them. Everyone will be happier.

2 − 10
SEX

Let me start here: This could, and probably will, be its own book.

Not all intensives are interested in sex, of course. Like everything in this book, sex is for some people more than others. But for those who like it, it can be not just a source of pleasure and connection but a tremendous resource.

When we love sex, we *love* sex.

We love diving in. We love long—hours-long—lovemaking, interrupted only by bathroom breaks and punctuated by snacks that are as good as the sex. We love fast, hard, intense sex, long or short. We love making out, we love soaking it in, we love sex, and of course we want it intense.

Intensives are deep and complex and more paradoxical on average than our expansive friends and colleagues. We've learned to embrace the paradox—to love it, even. But that doesn't make it any less present. And it's *especially* present in bed.

(I will often say "in bed" where what I mean is "in bed, or on the kitchen counter, or the dining room table, or in the woods by that big tree, or in the alley behind that one dive bar..." Because we are *amazing* about sex. When not buried under five thousand years of erotophobia, we *rock* the sexual experience.)

What makes intensives good at sex?

We have focus. We can pour ourselves into a single activity for a long period of time. We often read people very closely. But most importantly, we enjoy intensity. Generally speaking, we don't shy away from big experiences.

Sex is *supposed* to be a big experience. It doesn't always manage that, but our culture tells us it *should* be. And intensives seek out big experiences. We move toward them deliberately and consistently. So when something feels like eroticism and turn-on and *yum*, we go right to the front of the room. "Sign me up!"

Expansive partners sometimes get it and sometimes don't, but because sex is one of the rare places in our world that's actually coded for intensity, this is one of those places where we're likely to connect well with expansives, even if they don't get intensity at ALL the rest of the time. People *expect* sex to be intense. In fact, this is sometimes how we end up in relationships with expansives who aren't really ready or willing to have an intensive partner. The sex is *awesome*. So when you say you're having intensive-style, deeply engaged, blow-the-roof-off sex, for once no one says, "Wow, that's really a lot," while backing away slowly. Instead they wonder how they can get some.

It's a nice change of pace.

Here's what we tend to do:

- We learn our partners' bodies.
- We are very responsive to touch.
- We are playful.

- We are experimental.

- We tend to be "good, giving, and game" (that term comes from sex columnist Dan Savage and refers to a partner who practices to be good at sex, sometimes does stuff because their partner enjoys it, and is game to try new things).

- We believe there's more, so we go looking for it, which means the sex gets better over time if we're given free rein.

- We're wired for whatever we pay attention to, so when we pay attention to learning a new partner or having excellent sex, our brains get better at those things. (This is true of everyone, but I think one of the things that makes us intensives is that our brains are faster to rewire.)

- We are adventurous.

- We are curious.

- We are deeply connected.

- We are alive and excited and hot and real and turned on and honest.

- If something isn't working, we will tell you.

- If something is working, you'll know.

- We are all-in. Of course we are. We're intensives.

Many of these are the same qualities that make us excellent partners.

The skin is one giant sex organ, and we know it. We know it because we encounter the world that way. So when we put ourselves in bed with lovers, we have an almost infinite playground.

If you're having sex as or with an intensive:

Expect deep, grinding cravings. Expect fierce kisses. Expect that moment when you feel like you're one being. Expect not to know whether to laugh or cry. Expect to think about them for days afterward. Expect to want things you never thought you'd like. Expect to open wider, push harder, be louder. Expect to hear noises from yourself that you've never made before. Expect your world to be upended. Expect to cry and laugh and groan and beg and shout. Expect to be up against a wall, in the shower, on the living room floor, and at least once in a semi-public place. Expect to be turned on unexpectedly and all day. Expect to reimagine sex and what is sexy.

And if you are an intensive, expect to come out of it with a surplus of energy that feels like it could fuel the world.

For us, sex is more than just a connection, although it is that. It's a way for us to connect to our power. With sex we have access to a kind of primal energy, a primary energy source. It can feel like plugging into the sun.

Intensives who like sex tend to really like sex *a lot*. More frequently than most people do. Way above average. It comes and goes (that sine wave is everywhere) but when it's on, it's on. Three times a day isn't remotely unthinkable.

There are some things that make this possible. Creativity, for one. No one has to think of sex as limited to penetrative, genital engagement, but most people do. Expand your definition of sex, because there's a whole body to enjoy and you've got only so much friction before any given body part gets raw. We happily engage in all kinds of sex: Cyber. Phone. Manual. Various body parts with various other ones. If it turns you on, it might be sex. Intercourse is the tiniest fraction of what's out there. Our habit of thinking outside the box to get what we really want serves us exceedingly well here.

At root, being intensive in bed is like being intensive anywhere else.

Meh doesn't do it for us. We're either all-in or all-out. And we need places and partners that don't ask us to hold back, unless it's for the sake of building desire so that we're even hotter in the end.

So if we're on our game, we won't settle. We'll go for the best we can get.

We are not into junk-food sex. Good enough is not good enough. Mr. Right Now is kind of wrong, actually, unless he's a fantastic lover.

Because we are such sensorily focused people, and because we live in a world riddled by distance and disconnect, we may be in the habit of accepting junk food sex instead of intimacy, affection, and mindblowingly awesome sex. We may, in fact, never have had mindblowingly awesome sex. So we might think this is as good as it gets...in which case, we may also be people who don't really understand what the big deal is about sex, anyway. When the sex becomes mindblowing, then it gets our attention. Until then, who cares? We get a better high from doing our creative work of choice, or doing the work of our hearts, than we do from having mediocre sex.

If you're an intensive, you can't afford to settle.

The power you carry, the force, the joy, needs a place to land and focus. If you can't find a partner who can offer that (and return the favor), then your power and energy get dissipated instead of focused and nothing happens. You need a focuser, not a diffuser, which means you need a particular kind of power across the table from you.

The person you're with doesn't have to be an intensive, although it helps smooth the edges. But they do have to be able to handle big energy. And you have to have a deep enough connection that you're exchanging more than, as a friend of mine puts it, "wiggle wiggle wiggle pop."

Casual sex is fine, if eventually unfulfilling. The only real danger is that you get lulled into settling for just that. For partnership, though, you need to seek out something more.

The sex you are capable of in partnership is indescribable and can become a fuel source for all kinds of other things, creativity chief among them.

This is one of the places where we shine, if we let ourselves. Although sex can be anything—slow and sweet, sharp and aflame, loving or just straight-up fucking—there's an element of it that's always about intensity. Depth of connection or height of sensation or just feeling really, really, really good. We are awesome lovers. When we're smart, we tend to be very picky about who we take as lovers, too—which is brilliant.

If you want to take someone on as a project, put down the temptation and back away slowly. If you love someone so much you're ready and willing to help them learn, that's awesome. If you just want a great partner and lover, for God's sake, don't choose someone who isn't one. You may be so used to bad lovers that you don't know good ones exist.

They do.

Go find one.

Best way to find one? Step one: Start with you. Start feeling your fabulousness. Get in touch with how good it feels. Feel the sweet, seductive, powerful pleasure of your awesome. Step two: Go live your life and let the good lovers find you. And they *will* find you, as long as you are out living and not in, moping.

The fierceness and the joy that you can have with someone who matches you…

We want it all.

If we don't have it all, we're always looking, because we *know* there's something more out there.

And that always-looking state isn't fair to anyone. Not to you. Not to your partner. And not to anyone you might be interested in. Choose a partner or partners who delight in your power. If you feel like you're always holding back, talk about it and open that up, or find someone who's a better match.

Orgasm eluded me for decades.

It wasn't that I didn't want it.

It was just that I had no idea how to get there.

I was eventually very lucky to get exactly the help I needed with that. But somewhere along the line, running on a parallel but separate track, I was doing a similar thing with other kinds of pleasure (and power): I was sidestepping them at the last minute.

I was afraid to be loud. I was afraid to be seen. I was afraid to be foolish in public. I was afraid of *showing up*. I had my reasons. Visibility had turned out to be really dangerous for me for a long time.

But how it happened matters less than what happens now, which is this: I'm taking the cork out of this carbonated bottle of awesome, because there is *no reason* to cap my pleasure off. No reason to mute my laughter. No reason to not be utterly, completely, gleefully delighted.

This is what intensives *do*. We dive in and love the hell out of whatever we're loving, for real, completely, totally, thoroughly, and quite possibly with sound effects.

Why be shy about delight?

Why hide that you love something or someone *this much*?

That energy—in laughter, in pleasure, in unmitigated joy—is incredibly powerful. Once when some friends and I were discussing tantra and energy, we started discussing this thing called a kundalini awakening, which is basically what happens when you *really for real* unlock the incredible energetic power in your own body.

It can blow the top of your head off, metaphorically speaking. In fact, some stories exist about people doing it before they were ready and disrupting their psychological equilibrium quite a bit.

For better or for worse, my experience has been different from that of everyone else I was talking to. I've known that energy intimately from a very young age, so I've had a much gentler coming-to-terms-with-it. It didn't destroy me, but it deserves a healthy respect. Part of its root was always pleasure, but I was nervous about looking at it head-on—and sexual pleasure was even more confusing.

On the one hand, there was power there. I could feel it.

And there was pleasure there, which was delightful.

On the other hand, I felt like I wanted to *keep* the power I felt. I wanted to conserve it. I also wanted to hide it from everyone else. It felt like a secret weapon that lost efficacy if other people knew I had it.

I knew sexuality was Private. I also, marvelously, knew it was Okay. But definitely, absolutely Private.

But somehow the intersection of power, which felt like it needed some visibility, and sex, which felt like it needed to be hidden, got tangled.

So while I started masturbating very early in life, I couldn't find my way to orgasm.

What finally got me there was surrender.

2 – 11
THE VALUE OF SURRENDER

O nce we accept our delight, we open the door for everything else.

The advanced course is accepting what we can't control, accepting the fact that we can't control it, and learning to do things badly.

Surrender is perhaps one of the hardest things we do.

It's also one of the most vital.

It's hard to see at first, but we are much better at surrender than at control. Because we do well with thrills and calculated risks, we can take that flying leap and give the world permission to catch us on the way down. In fact, we do that like a superpower.

We need to do it. We need to practice it and love it and be okay with the inevitable occasional crash.

It's a huge part of who we are.

We look like irretrievable control freaks, and we are—about some things.

What we need to control is a fairly small wedge of the whole pie, however. We can roll with everything else, if we let ourselves do it.

The trouble is, we get in the habit of being in control. We get used to it. We try to stay in control of all the variables out of habit, mostly, not out of some sense of completeness of need. It's more a false sense of our identities, that we need to control everything because we said so.

It's a huge waste of energy. We aren't actually those people. We don't actually need to be in control of most of those things. In fact, we do much better when we lay a few plans and then *trust*.

We *can* let go.

Now, letting go is not intuitive. But it *is* glorious.

Step one: Decide what actually does matter. Make a list, because you will forget.

Step two: Find all the other things you're trying to control. Ask yourself how important they are. Odds are that if your kid eats a bologna sandwich every day for a year, nothing bad will happen.

Step three: Figure out how much distance you need to stop trying to control it. Do you need to stop making lunches so you stop trying to control what goes into the lunches? Do you need to drive the carpool or get a ride so you stop worrying about someone else's driving habits?

Step four: Direct your intensiveness toward surrender. This is the part where you turn things around. You can get the same high from surrender that you get from control. One may come easier to you than the other, and the one that's easier might be surrender, once you let go of the need to be in control all the time. Which one comes more easily doesn't really play into this process.

Especially for those of us for whom control is the primary modality, surrender is one of the most intense experiences available to us. Knowing what matters and what doesn't means that we can focus on the things that matter and let go all of the fiddly details that have been distracting us. Some of these details can simply be automated, either robotically or systemically: We can buy the same brand of toilet paper or always take the same route when we walk or automate our bill payments online. But there are things that can't be automated, like your kids' lunch. You might need to let go of control just so it doesn't have to be your problem. Bologna on white bread every day might be fine, or your kid might want to make elaborate lunches with smiley faces and carrots. It's probably all okay.

Of course, those are all things that don't really affect you. But things that *do* affect you can also be released. Let someone else figure out what to eat for dinner. If you're not into fashion and someone else in your family is, let them figure out what you should wear. Run a weeklong experiment and see how many things you can manage to not be in control of. Two weeks later, try to up the ante. You honestly need to control probably less than half of what you are in control of. If you live alone it's a little harder, but not impossible. Figure out who else could be in control and give control to them, if they're willing to accept it.

Of course, no discussion of surrender would be complete without talking about sex.

When I first started being sexually active I felt like I had to stay in control, at least of myself, at all times.

This was not a good strategy.

It served me well in some ways at first, but slowly it started getting in my way. It got in the way of pleasure, it got in the way of intimacy, it got in the way of relationships, and I would even say it made it harder to be in and express love. It took me literally decades to figure all this out. Along the way I had some inklings, but nothing clear. It was only by trial and error (and with some delightful partners) that I discovered how important surrender was.

If you feel like you always have to be in control of your own responses in bed, *stop it*. Sex is not about control. If you feel like you have to be in control of your partner's experience, *stop it*. Sex is not about control.

Now, if you like to play with power exchange, this has some flex. Certainly, if you're topping, you might need to be in charge of your partner's experience some of the time. I suggest that you also find a way to experiment with being on the other side, though. Bottoming is popular for a reason, and it's a great controlled, sandbox-type experience if letting go of control all at once is too hard.

Frankly, even if it's not your habit to play with power exchange, it might be worth having a conversation with your partner or partners about experimenting with it—not as a lifestyle change, but as a way for you to practice giving up control. It can be very interesting to find out what it takes for you to do that. Can you simply agreed to not be in charge, or do you need to have yourself tied so that you don't take over? Forcing yourself to give up control can in fact be a way of practicing self-control.

Notice, when you read erotica, to whom you relate. Notice, when you fantasize, which roles you prefer. Experiment with fantasies that shift your position. An absolutely essential word to the wise however, do not experiment with power if your gut tells you not to or with somebody you don't know well. In the kink scene people will often play with people they don't know very well but unless you have experience, don't start there.

And if you are really getting into it, *The Bottoming Book* and *The Topping Book*, both by Dossie Easton and Janet W. Hardy, are great resources.

There are a lot of places where the feelings that we associate with sex come in, even places that aren't sexual at all. Surrender can be one of those places. The brain chemistry that we experience in creativity and in sex (sex is, after all, a creative act) is also tied into surrender. When an artist is in flow, they are surrendered to the creative experience. When someone is having sex and is totally absorbed, they are surrendered to the sexual experience. For some people, meditation feels the same. Hypnosis can feel the same. Letting go is an amazing feeling.

What makes it un-amazing is the same thing that makes nervousness different from excitement: the narrative with which we frame the experience. The chemistry and the physical symptoms are very similar. But if I think I'm nervous, that's a bad thing; if I think I'm excited, that's a good thing. It has nothing to do with my internal systems, except insofar as my gut tells me whether this situation is good or bad. That's useful information, but if you have determined that there actually isn't a problem, then you are probably just making yourself unhappy when you don't need to be.

Where do you need to be responsible?

Where do you need to be restricted?

Challenge yourself. Are you sure?

When we do decide to let go, we're going to go all the way. That's how we relax. And that's how we fall in love.

2 – 12
TROUBLESHOOTING SEX

If your sex drive tanks: Something is wrong.

Maybe you're stressed.

You're emotionally off center with the person you're not wanting to have sex with.

You're emotionally off center with yourself.

You're sick.

Or you're on a hormonal rollercoaster (yes, this happens to all genders).

The most common culprit? Resentment and lack of connection.

The second most common culprit is overfamiliarity.

If you're feeling resentment, lack of connection, or generalized disrespect, try *Hold Me Tight* by Sue Johnson or *Passionate Marriage* by David Schnarch for fantastic tips.

If you're feeling overfamiliarity, try Esther Perel's *Mating in Captivity*.

If your life is too stressful, get yourself some support for changing the pattern. And if you're in the wrong relationship, get out before you damage things even more. A dip in sex drive can be just an incidental bump in the road, but for intensives it's really likely to be a canary in the coal mine.

We're not great at sex under stress. (Although the sex-in-foxholes thing, where you have sex with someone because you just made it through something huge and scary? We're great at that. Intensity piled on intensity: win.) We tend to be hypersensitive to changes in mood or situation, so if something goes "off" we're turned off, *poof.*

Good news: We can come back from it just as fast.

Bad news: We have to have something that's bringing us back.

Or maybe that's good news, too. Because the "something" bringing us back is vital. Without our own desire, sex is a dead loss for most of us. It keeps us real. It keeps us authentic. It keeps us aware of if and when we're faking it. That's not the *only* reason libido slips, but a missing libido is often a sign of something else amiss, and we are equipped with the super-deluxe notification model.

In a sex-averse culture, though, a high sex drive can feel like a burden, and we can "fix" the problem by allowing that turned-on feeling to ebb permanently. Then it's not in the way. It doesn't distract, it doesn't detract, and it certainly doesn't set us at odds with the culture that surrounds us or tempt us to do inappropriate things. Unfortunately, that doesn't solve the real problem. It just allows our stresses to pile up, unobserved, because after the first one the switch is off; there's nothing to tell us something is wrong. When you start insisting that you should feel pleasure, an alive, vibrant hum all the time, then you *know* when something is wrong. Because that vibrant hum isn't just about whether you want to have sex. It's about whether you are aware of your surroundings, of the energy of the people and places near you, of everything.

If you are "on," you can derive pleasure from the stars, from the breeze on your skin, from touching your pets, from clean sheets, from cool water in your mouth. If you are "off," even a beautiful and loving partner in your bed will barely scratch the surface.

Sometimes, no matter what you're into, you're going to have to stop doing it. Maybe it's sex and you're too sore to keep going. Maybe it's work and you have to wait for someone else's piece of the puzzle. This is where distraction becomes absolutely your best friend—but your *other* best friend is sublimation.

Now.

Sublimation gets a bad rap. Usually people talk about taking whatever they think they shouldn't be doing or wanting and shoving it so far down inside them that it accidentally squeezes out their ass and they end up shitting on someone because of it. This is *not* what I mean.

Sublimation, in *this* case, is where you take something yummy— like, let's say, a hypertuned sex drive—and you step it sideways, consciously and carefully, to something similar where it can get some relief, perhaps to creativity of a different kind.

I'm not recommending this if you're actively working to get your sex drive back or if your partner is ready for more sex. But if you've got sex drive to burn for any reason, sublimation can make your sex drive a huge gift.

PART THREE

WORK

3 – 1
WORK LIKE HELL, REST LIKE YOU'RE DEAD

The most important thing to know, the heart of intensive work patterns, is that we work like mad and rest like we're dead.

Give an intensive and an expansive the same month-long project.

The expansive will set aside two hours a day every day until the project is done.

The intensive will do the work in three nonstop, eat-sleep-breathe-work days (either at the beginning or right up against the deadline) and sleep the rest of the month.

That's just how we roll.

Everything else unfolds from that.

It's important to note that, although we are more hares than tortoises, there are times when the tortoise method works best, even if we don't like it. A huge part of the question is: *Can* we get the thing done in one burst of work?

If we can't, then we might need to go with slow and steady. This is not intuitive. The secret is for it to feel almost invisible. I don't take four- and five-hour chunks of time to write unless I have a very specific thing that seizes me. Instead, this book is getting written in half-hours and hours tucked in between dawn and sunrise. I wake up and type before leaving the bed, using a keyboard and my phone. I use few lights and interrupt my thoughts as little as possible. Just me, the writing, and that time in the morning when I'm lying in bed and thinking anyway.

It helps that I'm a morning person and that thinking wakes me up, but nonetheless, this book is getting written in a discipline of instants. I love getting something done so early that the whole day still unfolds before me. Unfortunately, sometimes I'm too sleepy to do anything more, but it doesn't matter. That brief time in the morning is so generative for me that I feel like I can afford to take the rest of the day "off." If the weather were nicer I'd nap on the beach, but it's November already. This thinking has been going on for nine months, and the book is ready to be born as the year turns to darkness. I'm okay with that.

When we're in work mode, we dive into a project headlong. We forget to eat. We forget to sleep. We ignore our kids, our partners, and our hobbies (sorry, y'all).

We don't mean to. But when we get started, our brains lock onto a target and will not let go. Drag us out for dinner, we'll start talking about our project. Take us to a movie, we'll see it as a metaphor for our project. Tell us about any problem you're having or any question you're considering or any major cultural event and we will find a way that our project solves your problem. (Just ask my friends how I've been since I started writing this book. Seriously.) The best strategy is for everyone to leave us alone. We will do the thing, take two days to detox, and then emerge from the cocoon and want to sleep and play and laugh and completely forget that work exists. There was a study on vacations once that found it takes you two weeks to actually get to a "vacation state" in your brain. Intensives know this.

The challenge is that this isn't how our world is built. Our world is built around discrete little building blocks of work that look the same every day, all week, all month, all year. Our schools and our businesses are built for expansives. No one expects someone to turn their whole life over to one project and then emerge, drooling and red-eyed, four days later, needing Gatorade and two weeks to sleep.

Well, almost no one.

St. John's College has students undertake one class at a time. They get it. They must.

Trimester schools, which let you do three classes instead of four or five, sort of get it.

Simon's Rock of Bard, which crams two years of high school and two years of college into one two-year period, gets it.

Commercial kitchens, stock trading floors, a lot of startups and coding environments, serious computer gamers, some newsrooms, hospital emergency rooms—some places do get it.

Lots of places, most places, most jobs don't.

Eventually it gets to us. Eventually we quit, or we stop focusing and lose our jobs. We look great on paper, until we fail to follow through because we got bored after the training period was over. Not enough intensity, not enough novelty. We're intensives; we need to be intensives. When we can't be, we're just not the best employees.

Looking for middle management? Look for expansives.

Looking for innovators who will rocket to the top? Hire an intensive, but for God's sake don't expect them to toe the line. Just keep them moving so no one ends up resenting them.

Looking for *intra*preneurs? That's the best way to integrate intensives into the conventional workplace. Give them a way to be an entrepreneur with a salary. But remember,: borders, boundaries, and rules are for other people. If your company culture can't tolerate that, don't hire intensives—and you'll have to do your own innovation.

Here's the trick: You can't have it both ways. If you want intensives in your company, you're going to need to give them wiggle room so they can continue being intensive. Hire them for their fire and innovation and then try to micromanage them, and you're going to lose everything you think you're paying for.

How to employ an intensive:

- Hire them on salary.

- Give them lots of schedule flexibility.

- Make sure they're working on something they're passionate about.

- Expect innovation.

- Let them rest after a big push.

- Reward and recognize them for their contributions.

- Offload the tasks they don't do well that are tripping them up. Let them focus where they shine.

When I was in college, I noticed something: the best pranks were pulled by the smartest students. They were also the hardest pranks to undo. I heard about an MIT prank that involved putting a car on top of a domed building. At Carleton, students moved a really large, awkward sculpture clear across campus and installed it on the concert-hall stage. A few years ago, some other Carleton students turned an observatory into R2D2 for April Fools' Day.

No one got hurt.

Nothing was damaged.

But the ability to plan and execute a really clever, really fun prank relies heavily on being bored. Really, really bored. And smart.

And intense.

We intensives want to be completely engaged. We want to be stretched to the edges of possibility, wrung out, and totally, completely absorbed and challenged by our work. The minute our work fails to keep up with the go-go-go pace of our brains, we get distracted and bored and start looking for something else to do. Anything else. It almost doesn't matter what.

This is how we torpedo our lives and our relationships and everything else that matters to us. We are *brilliant* when we are focused, but we need big things, intense things, to keep us focused. Most of what we're offered by default is not nearly big enough.

So we have to go out and make something else happen, because we get bored. We expand, we reach out, we take huge risks—sometimes too big.

We are border collies. Without a herd of sheep or chickens or ducks or something, we get ourselves in trouble. We need a project. And that's tricky.

We've been told all our lives that we're too much, too big. We've spent years learning that, years learning to shrink, years learning to be smaller and fit into a tiny space. And then we turn it around. There's that shining moment when we realize what we've been doing to each other and we decide to take a different path. We flip it around and start expanding and growing, occupying space and then more space, letting ourselves unfurl.

After so much constriction, it feels *great*.

And we, predictably (we are intensives, after all) take the expansion as far as it can go, and then a little farther. (You know, that moment when you look back and say, "Oh, the line was back there, the one I crossed"?)

Knowing where the line is *as you approach it*—now, that's the real trick.

Fortunately, we're good at tricks. We can learn this. It starts, necessarily and completely, with us. Our bodies. Our hearts. Our guts and intuitions and flesh and bones.

We likely don't know how to feel anymore.

We have learned to stop feeling, to ignore the feelings, to be sensible and rational…and it hasn't gotten us anywhere.

Around the time we stop shrinking and start expanding, we also notice that intuition works better than logic. Usually there's an adjustment period wherein we argue with ourselves about the illogic of following gut instead of data. Then we realize that we don't care about illogic, as long as it works. And *then* we have to convince the people around us that we're not crazy (or we think we have to).

Once we've thrown our proverbial hats in the ring, though, we have the opportunity to stop arguing and look around. We discover that the people who have done the things we most admire were called crazy by the people around them, that they made decisions no one understood—sometimes ever, certainly at the time—and that they went on to be brilliant.

As Henry Ford said, "If I had asked the people what they wanted, they would have said, 'faster horses.'"

No one could understand the idea of a car until someone put it in front of them; no one could see how much it would change the culture of the world until it *happened*.

We know the consequences of our actions are often not predictable. We *want* to be able to predict them, but we can't. We *want* to be in control of the outcomes, but we aren't. And we eventually learn that the nimblest posture is the safest. We don't know what is going to happen next, but we can know that we can roll with it—and not just stay standing, but dance.

We dance as the world shifts under us.

It's our specialty.

And we discover that balance, survival, staying upright all rely on the same thing: on our bodies, on us being aware and awake and brilliant and delighted, yes, but also knowing what the feelings are—the sensations, the concrete in-our-bodies-ness. Those matter, too. They matter a *lot*. In fact, they turn out to be the root of knowing what our intuition is saying.

Our biggest bugaboo is one of our strongest assets: We like everything to be perfect. But we can get mired in that quest for perfection if we don't listen to our bodies.

We have to write first and ask questions later.

Fortunately, this is our first and most intuitive way to work. We learn early in life to slow down and think things through, convinced that *that* is the route to perfection. We learn this from the people around us, most of whom do not have the gut instincts we do or choose not to use what they have.

Our guts are our best routes to perfection, but by the time we are adults, even *we* don't even believe that. The people around us don't believe it either—mostly because we don't, but also because everyone is stewed in the same mix of disbelief and the weird work ethic that honors discomfort and struggle over pleasure and ease.

3 – 2
PERFECTIONISM

For me, and many people, intensiveness means that I dive *right* into whatever I'm doing. (This is kind of funny, because I still have a fear of diving that prevents me from going headfirst into the water, pretty much ever. Working on it. Not there yet. Anyway...)

I dive in. Both feet. Sometimes I tell myself I'm going to Do This Forever, but that's only true in rotation with the other hundred and fifty million or so things I'm interested in. I never lose interest, I just keep adding things. (Intense learner, yep, that's me.)

I *love* that I'm intense about learning. But what gets in my way is when I decide that if I'm going to learn this, it's going to be *perfect*.

I'm going to be the best. I'm going to *learn all the things* and do them at a paraprofessional level, so help me heaven and earth.

All this does is *stress me out*. I'm used to high levels of adrenaline and cortisol, for a bunch of unfortunate reasons, so my body tends to lean in that direction anyway—but there is no reason on earth that I have to do it to myself.

(Also, adrenaline and cortisol fuck with functions like short-term memory, so if you're stressed at a networking meeting or a birthday party, you're screwed.)

When I decide that I'm going to do it *perfectly* that leads directly to...

Not doing it at all.

That's right. Perfectionism leads to procrastination. ARGH. So I've had to learn to be intensely laid back.

Um?

It works like this: I can do as much or as little of this thing as I want to. I can do it badly. I never have to show it to anyone if I don't want to. It totally helps. I've even designated a few creative activities (painting and drawing) as things I am *allowed* to do badly. I'm even *supposed* to do them badly. If I do them well, it's a total accident.

As intensives, we need permission, support, and guidance about how to be less intense when it's not working for us. Perfectionism does not usually work for us. When it works, it works. But sometimes you just have to do something for sheer joy. Do it for the pleasure of the feeling of the brush loaded with paint gliding across the paper.

We need to let ourselves play. Let ourselves scribble. Let ourselves be wrong.

We need to write first, ask questions later.

That's what I posted to Twitter this morning, but really, it could be tattooed on the inside of my eyelids.

Do whatever thing is calling you. Ask questions later. Do not pass go. Do not collect $200. Go directly to your keyboard or studio or canvas or drawing board or flowchart or equation or chalkboard.

Go. Just *go*.

I brushed my teeth and took my morning supplements, and I went to the bathroom. I also put in my contacts. That was a lot, indulgent, more than usual, but I wanted to brush my teeth and my toothbrush is supposed to live in the fridge to remind me to take my pills....

And it wasn't worth overthinking. I woke up thinking, "write first, ask questions later," and even though I didn't have a clue why today that was the thought, even though I said out loud last night that I might give myself the day off from writing today, here I am, fifteen minutes after my eyes opened, fingers on keyboard.

Write first, ask questions later.

Why?

Because "write first, ask questions later" is the way things get done.

Intensives can overthink things. Intensives can overthink things so badly that we can't get anywhere or do anything because we are trying so damn hard to get it right and we can see all the options. *All* of them. We can also talk ourselves into—or out of—*anything*, with the result that even though we want to do *everything*, we often get completely mired.

There are two options. One is to have so many projects going that the research phase for one thing is simultaneously the action phase for something else. That works fine if you're an expansive. But intensives tend to lose interest fast and move on to something else. So the other option is to just leap, before anyone can get too thoughtful about it.

This obviously has its risks. "Look before you leap" has been a maxim for hundreds of years for a reason. But we learn to trust our guts, to trust our subconscious to get what our conscious, thinking minds can only sort of imagine. We learn to "just know" instead of trying to figure it out. Justification and explanation are our enemies.

This also means that we have to train long and hard in the things that matter to us. If you care about social justice, as an intensive you are better off reading a lot about social justice and surrounding yourself with social-justice activists. Why? Because you won't sit down and carefully list and analyze the impact of your next major decision with regard to class or race or disability. You'll just leap. But your gut will tell you when you're off—if it *knows* when you're off. Make those things enough a part of your landscape and you won't have to think before you begin. You will still need to analyze as it develops, ask questions, and engage with people to help you stay on track. But the very beginning will feel off if it's off, and you won't do it. Will you screw up royally sometimes? Yes, no lie. *But* you will figure it out and get back on track. So if something matters to you—environmentalism, antiracism, your kids, communication skills, gun laws, cheap oil, frugality, modesty—immerse yourself in it enough that it becomes second nature. Just don't forget how to let your thinking evolve, and don't be surprised when support comes from unexpected places.

3 – 3
CULTURE SHOCK

I have long had an interest in creating my own…well, everything. Clothes, food, furniture, the basics of life as we know it. Years ago, before Facebook but after newsgroups, when reading blogs was most of what the online world was doing, I ran across a blog with a wealth of information and a philosophy that was like mine, but taken to a logical extreme. The family was homesteading in the Pacific Northwest and did almost everything for themselves and for very little money. It was really fascinating.

My politics were almost completely the opposite of this family's, but we had so much in common that it built a bridge for me. I still follow them (now also on Facebook) and I like to think that, should we ever meet, we could delight in each other and our shared valuing of things made at home, by hand, naturally; foods that are healthy and whole and healing; strong families; and loving connections. I like to think the rest of it would be like any other cultural exchange.

That's where the piece about obedience and submission versus Breaking All The Rules comes in really handy. When we meet someone with whom we disagree, we tend to have an impulse to *be right*. I want to be *right*, dammit. And if I just explain long and well enough, the person I'm talking to will agree with me...*poof!* Right? (Not really. But an intensive can dream.)

On the other hand, when I visit another culture I'm pretty good about observing the Prime Directive, live-and-let-live, submitting to the conditions of the culture I'm visiting. Mostly. The better I am, the better things go. I highly value being respectful of cultures I'm visiting, whether across the street or across the world. I don't have to agree with them, and there are limits of human rights and decency. But I work really hard to check my assumptions and biases at the door. That's important. Assumptions and biases can stop learning in its tracks and replace it with judgment. We intensives are *really good* at judging people. Usually that's not helpful. At all. Which means we need to not do it. Which means turning that rule-detecting, submission-to-what-we-don't-understand talent *way* up.

Leave an antenna up just in case something is dangerous. But don't let your initial detections of something strange turn into a resistance that blocks you from seeing what's really happening.

Take the issue of hijabs, for example. Lots of Westerners have been in the habit of assuming that hijabi women are oppressed, that they are forced to wear the hijab by a misogynistic culture or relative.

Often that's not true. But if you weren't raised with the hijab, you've got to be willing to entertain something that's foreign to you with a completely open mind, making no judgments. None. Not even a little one.

That's a leap, because your intuition might be going nuts based on what you think it would be like for *you* to wear a hijab. Because it's not appropriate for you to just run an experiment and find out what it's like, you have to approach the question open-mindedly and then maybe find some resources that will tell you more about what it's like from the inside.

And then you have to submit, because you have to believe hijabi women—the ones who are reporting from the field. No matter how good your intuition usually is, in this case you don't get to override what you're being told. Hijabs don't mean what Western culture often makes them mean.

Conversely, if modesty is really important to you, that doesn't mean you get to intuit that people who prefer nakedness or scant clothing are necessarily immoral or even that they like sex. They might. But it doesn't always mean what you think it means.

We tend to jump to conclusions. Mostly that's great; it gets us moving before thinking can mire us down. But when we're guests, it's a whole different ball game.

What does cultural competence have to do with work styles?

Intensive and expansive work styles arise from and foster different work cultures. The more your style is similar to—or at least accepting of—the work culture in which you're embedded, the easier life will be.

There are certain professions where intensiveness is the baseline behavior. Professional kitchens are intensive spaces; professional theater is an intensive space. We expect the people who work there to be intensive, and if you're not intensive they think you're little weird. Maybe you don't care, but in corporate America, if you want to rise through the ranks you need to manage your intensiveness so it's barely visible.

Work compatibility doesn't have to be about squishing anybody—you or another person or the group. It *is* about recognizing the various cultures that we carry, even when they have nothing to do with countries of origin and everything to do with who we (and our departments and our companies) are. Making cultural transitions and building cultural bridges is key to living happily and gracefully as an intensive. We have to be able to see cultures and their influence on us—and on everyone else.

3 – 4
Leap...
and Build the Net

E ither we leap or we get stuck.

One of the cultural characteristics intensives have to deal with in a work environment is the speed with which an idea becomes action. Because we like perfection, we can get mired in the details fairly easily, which means we can be prone to decision paralysis. The remedy tends to make expansives (and expansive cultural spaces) really nervous: We need to act when we get a chance and an inspiration, even if it's a leap of faith.

When we're not hyper-focused on one thing, there are so many things we want to do that the hardest part is a lack of hours in the day. Things like illness and sleep deprivation only make it worse. Everyone needs sleep, but we need it more than everyone else—because we need every minute we can get.

Write first, ask questions later, and dive into the rabbit holes. Just go.

You may have heard of "rabbit holes": When you get on the Internet to look for something and three hours later you realize that you've been following one link after another into a topic you never knew you had to know all about, until just now. It feels rather like Alice's long, strange fall down the rabbit hole at the beginning of *Alice in Wonderland.*

Intensives are the royalty of rabbit-hole followers. We will start out researching pot-roast recipes and end up investigating sustainable-farming practices in Nepal, which will lead us down a long line of inquiry regarding traditional Nepali building construction, which will send us to the aftermath of the recent earthquake, which will land us squarely in seismic-detection technology, which will lead us to nuclear-weapons testing in the Middle East...

And all of it will be fascinating, and a remarkable amount of it will stick in our heads, especially considering that many of us can't remember the names of people we've been introduced to five minutes after the introduction has been made. It often seems like we know something about everything but nothing is very useful—*until* we start communicating with the people around us.

Our brains make leaps and connections that a lot of brains don't. We tend to understand things intuitively and trust our intuition where others would question it. That means we have to find ways to explain what we are thinking. This should be easy: Just say it, that's what language is for. Unfortunately, that's not how it works.

Me: "So I was thinking that if X is true, then probably Y, Z, and Q are also true, and that means that we can use the tools we use on X on Y and Z but probably not Q because of these exceptions."

Expansive friend: "Umm... How did that go again? And what do those exceptions have to do with Q, much less with the tools we use on X?"

I'm left thinking, *Damn, I thought it was obvious.* But I've made some leaps and expected my friend to follow. Instead, I have to help my expansive friend understand how I got there.

Me: "So I was thinking that if X is true, then probably Y, Z, and Q are also true, and that means that we can use the tools we use on X on Y and Z but probably not Q because of these exceptions."

Expansive friend who is obsessed with woodworking: "Huh?"

Me: "It's like trying to fix a dresser that's racking. You'd fix it with a diagonal brace somewhere, right?"

Friend: "Yes..."

Me: "So if a diagonal brace fixes a dresser that's racking, then diagonals and triangles probably stabilize almost anything. So we can use a triangle cleat to stabilize a roof truss, too. And if the triangle cleat works, that means the diagonal doesn't have to go the full diagonal, just a tiny corner—except when the racking forces are too strong to withstand, because long levers exert more force."

Friend: "*Oh!* But—"

Me: "So X is the diagonal brace on the dresser, and Y and Z are the roof truss, but Q won't work because it's like the long-levers problem. We need a different solution for Q."

Friend: "Well, what if we...."

Problem solved. (Your metaphors may vary.)

We learn to do this early, because if we don't do it, nobody understands us and we can't communicate our ideas.

Of course, when we *do* it, people think we're outlandishly optimistic or pessimistic.

Which we are.

Sometimes one, sometimes the other. It keeps the world in balance.

3 – 5
SUCCESS

When intensives succeed, what does it look like?

First of all, we tend to ignore what everyone around us thinks. We succeed or fail by our own standards—which, unless we've trained ourselves out of it, can be incredibly high. We don't just want to *attend* the benefit dinner, we want to sell out a whole table or two. We don't just want to *speak* the language, we want to be mistaken for a native speaker. We don't just want to *run* a marathon, we want to place.

Actual success is a lot broader, but we have a tendency not to give ourselves credit. When we get close to the ideal, we've still succeeded, and we really benefit from recognizing that.

If your goal was to make $1,200 and you made $1,180, that's still *awesome*. If you are able to carry on conversations about politics in Portuguese, you *still learned the language*, even if you have an accent. If you ran a marathon at *all*, that's 26.2 miles. *Own it.*

My editor Sarah Grey's intensive kid understands this to the bone.

Sarah: I'm settling in for a bedtime story with my six-year-old and I ask her if she'd like to read it to me. She's reading ahead of her grade level and really starting to enjoy it for the stories. She's game.

She reads the entire book aloud, indicating with a wave of her hand when she wants me to fill in a particularly tricky word. I don't say a word otherwise, since that will only make her mad. Once or twice I think she's waving when she's scratching her nose and provide a word-- producing a snarl-- but for the most part it goes well. She makes it all the way through the book without getting mad.

After she's done, I congratulate her on doing a great job. She frowns. "You read most of it."

"Dude. I only read a few words. You read the whole thing! Give yourself some credit!"

"No," she says, crawling into bed. "I am never gonna give myself credit ever in my LIFE."

By failing to acknowledge our successes, we can deny ourselves the sweet little hit of brain chemistry that comes from accomplishment. Over time, we stop being motivated to try, because we train ourselves that unless we're *super amazing* we don't get the hit. We fail to condition ourselves for attempts at things we know are stretches—and, being intensives, everything we *really* want is a stretch somehow, because we want to be *fucking awesome amen.*

There's another side to this. We learn that we can show up halfway, phone it in, and still be fine by most people's standards. We constantly disappoint ourselves when we're out of integrity like that, though, and *that* means that we really can't afford to do jobs that don't resonate with us. Our standards fall, our engagement falls, and then we get down on ourselves for doing a shitty job. Then we don't trust ourselves. And sometimes we get fired, because people *do* eventually notice. And remember what I said about trust being imperative, because we like to jump out of planes? Not trusting ourselves is about eighty billion times worse than not trusting others. We *have* to trust ourselves. The minute you see yourself starting to mistrust your *own* commitments, promises, reliability, or capacity, GTFO (get the fuck out). Do whatever you have to do to change that. As intensives, we can't afford that kind of slippage, because it affects our ability to do anything at all.

Sometimes that means setting strict limits or rules for ourselves— but unless the depression monster has got us by the throat, that actually feels kind of good. And, often, all-or-nothing rules are easier than sort-of-kind-of-maybe rules.

For example: Let's suppose that you have a Thing you do at 8 AM every day, and it makes the rest of the day awesome. You know you need it to perform at peak. You know you need to perform at peak because you're an intensive, so you're in a job that demands that of you. However, in order to do that 8 AM thing, you have to be in bed with your eyes closed by 10 PM.

It's probably easier to set yourself a bedtime of 10 PM *every single day* (except on special occasions) than it is to say 10 PM every weekday. If you slip, then you probably stay slipped for a while, so the stakes are high.

You also have to allow for reality, even if you hate authority. That's for two reasons: one, sometimes you can't meet the commitment without betraying a bigger one, like if finishing the race means running on an injury and you have a commitment (I hope!) to self-care. Two, sometimes something bigger or better will happen if you're flexible. You hate doing stuff that doesn't make any sense, and sometimes the not-making-sense shows up midstream. If something needs adjusting, adjust it.

But hitting that 10 PM goal on the nose, night after night, feeds your "accomplishment" brain chemistry. You begin to trust yourself to show up and keep commitments. And that lets you trust yourself for bigger things.

And how do intensives celebrate those successes?

Typically, we don't.

That's right. Even though we get *super* excited and work like hell on the Thing of the Moment, by the time we complete it, we tend to be on to the next thing with little or no attention for the last thing. This is a nasty side effect of the 80 percent problem. *It is also foolish.* I know we don't mean it—we're just *so* excited for the *next* thing we've been daydreaming about. But again, we need the hit of success chemistry in the brain. *We did it!* Even if we think it should have been easier, or even if it *was* easy, we still need to take a minute and say:

YAY!

TA DA!

As kids we were often told, either explicitly or implicitly, that we were taking up too much space, demanding too much attention, or being self-centered, so we learned not to call attention to our successes. And we are especially prone to blow off accomplishments that are easy for us because we're experts or talented in something—can't everyone do that?

Enough of that bullshit.

When you win, *sing it!* And if you notice that the people around you are not very comfortable with that celebration, call some intensive friends! We need all kinds of people, and we definitely need to include each other in that list. You'll know an intensive because they will cheer with you and then share something *they* just did that was *also* awesome!

Form celebration circles, where you get together and talk about how cool all your accomplishments are. Being able to celebrate openly will *change your brain.*

3 – 6

DON'T BURN
THE 10 PERCENT

Part of success is knowing when to stop. As intensives, we tend to move the goalposts—so when you get to 80 or 90 percent of the original task or goal, you add another 20 or maybe 50 percent, so you never actually *get there*.

Do not do this.

(If you have trained yourself not to do this, *go you!*)

Set a reasonable goal, and let it be met. Let it get there. Let yourself fully arrive. And then shut down the computer, turn around and run home, put down the pen. *Be. Done.*

Rest. Relax. Celebrate.

The need to rest after an intense burst of work is very real and critical to your continued success. If you do not rest at an appropriate time, you will wake up with the creativity and generative equivalent of a hangover and you will feel like shit for three days and you will have a deep, inexplicable resistance to diving into your next project. Of course, your subconscious knows *exactly* what it is avoiding.

Pacing yourself is *not* an intensive trait, so you need to make it happen in an intensive-friendly way. Let yourself run full-out. Let yourself get tired. Get exhausted, even. But *stop before you're totally depleted.* Leave 10 or 15 percent in the tank. But here's the trick: *Act* like you're totally depleted. Don't convince yourself that, since you're not utterly flattened, it would be okay to do laundry and build a chicken coop before bed. *It is not.* Ten or 15 percent *is* totally depleted. Give yourself the full restorative treatment and you'll be on your feet the next day. It makes a *huge* difference. Burning that extra 10 percent costs you *days* of function.

This is a hard lesson to learn, especially when you're "in the flow" and can't really feel the depletion. Working nonstop is one of our Things. It sometimes takes a while for us to get into the flow, and once we do it feels so awesome we don't want to get out of it for any reason whatsoever. Learning how to monitor your body sensations while staying in the flow is kind of like learning to meditate, or play piano, or pat your head and rub your belly. It is an incredibly useful skill and one worth developing, because the alternative is a feast-famine cycle that not only depletes you but affects all of your close relationships. You are too tapped at the end of the day to engage meaningfully, which means that you don't make those deep connections with the people who matter to you, which means that the relationships suffer or even end. It's incredibly damaging, and you *cannot* just power through it.

This goes double if you're using your intensiveness to power through something you don't actually like doing, or a long string of hard work. Do *not* burn the 10 percent—it will cost you.

3 – 7
FAILURE

What does it look like when an intensive fails?

We are, by our nature, big thinkers and we often are big riskers. So it follows that our failures are also, often, epic.

Since we are *also* often perfectionists, this can take some getting used to.

Allowing for failure as part of the process is central. Thank goodness for the iterative programming model. *Iterative development* comes to us from the IT/programming world, which often harbors fugitive intensives from elsewhere in corporate culture. *Iteration* means that instead of trying to get an idea to be perfect the first time, we can take the inspiration, run with it, offer a rough draft, edit, draft, edit, and not get emotionally attached to something until it has actually been refined to the point where we (*even we*) can be proud of it.

Here's the thing. When we take a project all the way to what we think is "complete," we're not terribly receptive to feedback. We see potential like other people see reality, and we tend to drive toward whatever it is we see with a fierceness and passion that's hard to counterbalance.

Which is not to say that we shouldn't see that vision! We should, absolutely. But we are also sensible, flexible people. We can see when there's a better path emerging. Our willingness to change course is largely a function of how attached we are to the initial vision. Which is to say, we do better when we're not too attached, when we still see the vision as a flexible, malleable thing.

Failure is not a problem.

Let me repeat that: *Failure is NOT a problem.* Failure can be epic and messy and we do better when we plan for it, but it is definitely not a problem.

3 – 8

INTENSIVES AND INJURY

We have, as in most things, two directions we go when we get injured. Either we ignore it, push ourselves, and leave the hospital against medical advice, or we become extra careful and cautious, making every move as though it might be our last, resting *hard*.

There is a middle ground, but it's hard to find. Ordinarily, just listening to our bodies would provide that middle space, where (regardless of the doctors) what feels like a good place to start is a good place to start, and continuing feels right at a certain point, so we continue. However, sometimes recovery requires pushing through some pain and going past some things that feel like limits. Recovering faster is actually sometimes better for you. But you probably need a physical therapist to help you with it, to figure out where the line between productive and unproductive pain is.

Because we are used to being really good at things. Including getting better.

Or else we are used to being really bad at things that look even vaguely athletic.

Whichever story we tell about ourselves and being sick or injured, it will be true, because intensives are much more belief-driven than other people. Sure, we like to think we're all rational and shit, a lot of the time, but mostly we get our reality from what we believe— and if reality isn't in line with that, we swing it around until it agrees with us.

We can believe things so hard that they come true, just like that. And if *that* doesn't work, we believe harder.

Now, I'm not saying we can bring people back from the dead or anything. But I *am* saying that if we believe something, especially about ourselves, it tends to become a self-fulfilling prophesy.

Nowhere is this truer than in the realm of health.

We can really get in the way of our own recovery—and we can *stop* getting in our own way.

If we push ourselves too hard, which we can do almost without thinking about it, we become tremendously focused on some external goal we set: being able to walk to a certain place or stand up by a certain date or think or move or whatever. We hate to admit that we might heal on the same schedule as everyone else. When you wrap your identity around the armature of meeting a goal, you will do almost anything to meet that goal, because it becomes not something you can or can't *do*, but who you *are*.

And who you are is a very, *very* big deal.

Your brain is very attached to who you think you are.

That's why the question "Who do you think you are?" is so devastating. It implies that whatever you are doing is incompatible (and too elevated) for who the speaker thinks you are. In that moment, the best defense is to remind yourself that you *do*, in fact, think you are a person who does those things, whatever they are.

But when you start to break the mold, there can be a little voice that says, "Who do you think you are?" *from the inside.* That's a much harder voice to ignore.

And yet—sometimes you have to admit that you are not Superman or Wonder Woman and you heal like everyone else heals, one cell at a time.

But: If you are accustomed to daring to think you are bigger than the voices around you and the voices in your head, that in itself becomes an identity, and failing to surpass all expectations is a contradiction of your identity. *Who do you think you are?* Oh, but you failed. You're just like everyone else after all.

Ouch.

So, when we are sick or injured, being sick or injured becomes a challenge to who we are after a while. We need to reconcile being extraordinary with being ordinary. We do not need to be special in all things to be ourselves.

In these times, identity-reinforcing people become vital to our healthy recovery, even more so than that physical therapist. Because if we feel that our identity is threatened, we *will* resist all the medical advice in the world, or make ourselves special by *not* healing (going from one extreme to the other and embedding being injured into our identity).

So we need all the people who know and love us to gather around and love us for who we know ourselves to be, even as we are not acting like that person regarding our injury or the problems we are having. We need reassurance and support that we *are* intense and extraordinary, with or without whatever state of abled-ness we've got.

This might seem like unwise ego-pandering to those watching from the outside. People might say, "You really need to get used to the limitations of your new condition," blah blah blah. But what they don't understand is that this one limitation does not mean the rest of the body or mind are limited. This is a perennial problem for all kinds of disabled people. People often find that their one disability leaves people thinking that they are helpless in all arenas, like when people shout at wheelchair users or speak very slowly to blind people. That's bullshit. Whether your disability is temporary or permanent, it has a limited scope.

What's more, even if you *are* more limited, now is not always the time to talk about that. Acute recovery can be a time to use the mind as a shaping tool. *What people believe* has been shown in study after study to affect their ability to heal and recover. This is the time to reinforce anything that feels like strength—*if that feels in integrity for you.* Brains take in information at a rate that they can manage. Be there for people who are discovering that something isn't working, but give them all the support they need to believe it might work again, if they want to go that direction. If not, give them the support they are asking for. And if you're the one injured, ask for the support you need.

Those medical miracles you watch TED talks about? They are the result of absolutely impossible beliefs and determination and support. If you are the one injured, surround yourself with people who will believe you and believe in you. Accept what you have to but if your gut says something else, fight like hell, because it's yours. That possibility and that success belong to you, too.

3 – 9
INTENSIVES, RULES, AND POWER

This can go two ways.

One: We break the rules that are there and we write our own.

Really, we don't have much use for the rules other people write. We take them as suggestions, advice, information about what worked for someone else, challenges. But that's it.

That's what entrepreneurial intensives tend to look like. Also artists. And activists. ACT-UP and Black Lives Matter are movements led by intensives (although probably largely organized backstage by expansives). We break rules that don't suit us, and we tend to operate by a much different code—internal morality, if you will—things that we believe are right and good and useful. It doesn't matter much to us whether the establishment likes them or not.

We love to operate in a system which makes us feel like we have integrity with *something*. But we are unlikely to accept an external rule set unless we have really examined it and decided we believe it.

On the other hand, if someone breaks the rules that we have in our heads, we can get really irate. The classic unhelpful version of this is "Someone is wrong on the Internet."

Better to spend our energy elsewhere. Which we learn…and then take our energy to our own work, if we're smart.

Two: We take rules very seriously.

We hate breaking rules and we pride ourselves on going above and beyond to exceed the expectations of our superiors. That's what military, law enforcement, and teacher intensives tend to look like.

But if you scrape back a layer, you find that it's all the same.

Artists who are learning from someone they really like will cleave to the instruction like someone dying. Teachers trying to be extraordinary educators will play fast and loose with classroom conventions.

We hold paradox in our bones, and we do it easily. We want to Do It Right while being amazing and innovative.

Sometimes we get God complexes: We think we are saving the world, that we are better than the rulemakers and the legislators and the people who really do just follow the rules and collect a paycheck.

Sometimes we are. Mostly we can get ourselves into big trouble this way. If you have to break the rules where you are, you should be looking to *get out.*

You're right that world needs your innovation. But not like that. There are exceptions, of course. Social revolution, times when the whole system has to change and you're leading the charge from the inside. Killing the Don't Ask Don't Tell rules in the US military or changing segregation in the the Jim Crow South, yes. Innovative teachers fighting to educate our kids, yes. Don't stop. We need you. In those places, we're breaking the rules of law but cleaving to a higher order, a set of rules we believe supersedes them. When we are loyal to a person or a rule or a law or a principle, it tends to overrule everything.

But cops who kill people running away and teachers who tell kids they are stupid? There's no call for that. Intensiveness is not an excuse for brutality of any kind—although, if we pick the wrong thing to pledge allegiance to, it can lead there. Channel your intensiveness somewhere else instead. Focus it elsewhere. Allow yourself to be intense someplace where it makes things better. Stop soaking in avoidable fear.

Be especially wary of your rulebreaking if it takes advantage of the needy and vulnerable.

We are attracted to power, the people who have it and having it ourselves. In order to have it, we're willing to do the necessary for almost as long as it takes. In order to bask in the aura of people who have it, we're willing to toe a lot of uncomfortable lines.

But in the end, we have to be the ones who say, "Enough. I'm not doing it. I am not willing to go that far to feel powerful; I am not willing to go that far to feel someone else's power." We have to be that one guy in the picture who isn't saluting Hitler. That's not just our personality, it's our role in the world and our moral responsibility.

This power thing can also take us to other edges, like being kinky. The world of kink is a place where it's totally cool to want to do extreme things to engage with power, as long as everyone consents and no one gets permanently hurt.

There's nothing wrong with that.

Power is hot—at least, intensives tend to think so. We either hate or love it; often both, and when we don't it's often because we've suppressed feelings that didn't fit with the world we ended up in.

We also, it is worth noting, like power because it's damn efficient. It gets things done, and *that* is super-hot. Power means decisions get made, life moves on, people see results. We don't dilly-dally on one project long after it becomes uninteresting. Power means *go*. We *like* go. It means certainty, or getting to try something and iterate. It means clarity and direction. We can see the benefit of that. Even those of us who are very good at being in charge will often cede our power to someone else if that's the way to get things done.

We will have high standards for our leaders, but we'll definitely give them space to lead. Millennials in particular tend to be willing to do this and happy to see what power will bring. Boomers tend to be suspicious of power as a group, and Generation X inherited some of that suspicion without replacing power with anything useful. Those of us who grew up after the Boomers had a fair measure of difficulty being appreciated in our power. Today, as the Millennials parent, power is becoming a navigable, visible, and honorable force and it's becoming easier for intensives to find our place in the world. But we've spent two generations fighting leadership and power, so it's going to take a bit before power is reintegrated in a healthy way.

3 – 10

FALL FOR YOUR WORK

When I fell in love for the first time, I had no idea what was happening. I knew I was totally caught up in the experience and in the person I loved. I finally, *finally* figured out what love was.

When I fell for a project for the first time, it wasn't that different. Intensives fall hook, line, and sinker for things that are too big to be imagined. We get off on stretching our brains to accommodate new ideas. A dear friend and fellow intensive, when she was earning very little money as an intern, decided to attend a benefit dinner. Not one to settle for buying a seat or two, she committed to a whole *table*—and she filled it. It broke my brain a little; now when I suspect there's a bigger way to think about something, I ask myself, "What would she do?"

Our talents for cross-linking and metaphors also bring us to incredible places of integration. Tools that have historically been used for something are getting used for something else, and it's because we thought, "If X works here, why not there?" Sometimes it's so *obvious* that we wonder how it's possible that no one has thought to do that before, and sometimes it's such a surprise that it takes three days to really fully understand how it would work.

What's most important to know about our working is that our work is important. It's critical. And it is not worth less because we do it from this fierce, chaotic, wild place. We cannot work as effectively in other forms; we have to know that about ourselves and honor it.

When we choose methods that truly reflect us, that fit us, *then and only then* can we shunt aside enough make-work and energy drain to actually lead.

And when we lead, we lead *brilliantly*.

3 – 11
INTENSIVES IN
LEADERSHIP

Look around the world and you'll see intensives at the very tops of organizations, starting new ventures, running the nimblest and most unpredictable games in town.

We also create strong systems when we need to.

Many intensives love to be in charge. We love to control the big picture. We love to know it's going to be done right.

And this means that often—not always, but often—we love to lead.

Often we don't *know* we love to lead, because we had it squished out of us at a young age. We think we love lots of things, but leadership, maybe not. We probably got told to be quiet, sit down, and pay attention when we were children.

That doesn't encourage leadership.

It might have taken us twenty or thirty or forty or fifty years to notice that we actually liked to be loud and in charge.

If you are a cis straight white man between thirty and sixty, you are especially likely to have been encouraged to have opinions or be loud or take charge. Most intensives have not.

Fortunately, we haven't got much use for rules.

We can make logic look like it says anything. It's like statistics. That's why we only trust our guts in the end—because we know logic can be bought or bent. So we go into the Catholic Church, we go into the armed forces, we follow the rules strictly...and, eventually, we get frustrated. Now, the best-case scenario is that we're in a position of power—that our rule-following was good enough for long enough to allow us to help to shape the institution and change some of the things that are frustrating about it. Next best is that we recognize our frustration and we leave. We quit, we ask for an honorable discharge, we leave the church, whatever it is we need to do.

Unfortunately, that's not always the likely case. It's really hard for us to concede that we've made a mistake. We don't like to make mistakes, and joining a large institution that's very rule-bound is a pretty big mistake for intensives, especially when it affects your career. So we're unlikely to do the best possible thing, which is just to see it through to the next possible exit and leave gracefully.

Much more likely is that we will hang on and hang on and hang on, frustrated at our lack of power and getting more and more strict about the rules for ourselves and everyone else. When we're in a hierarchy and we're not at the top, we become very rigid because we're frustrated. We believe that somewhere in this institution is the level at which we are going to be free to say what we have to say and do the things we *know* are the best things, and until then we just have to hang on and wait.

But we're not good at just hanging out and waiting. Our frustration means that we spend our spare time becoming really anal-retentive about enforcing the rules that we're supposed to enforce, especially in dealing with people who are below us. As our intensiveness turns toward enforcement (since we can't use it for creativity) we become crabby and unpleasant—it's a bad situation.

Finally, we break. Now we start to bend the rules for ourselves, rationalizing and making up reasons why the rules shouldn't apply to us because we can't stand them anymore. We think—no, we *pretend* to think—that because we're at a certain level or have a certain role we don't have to follow the rules. It's not lying—we *actually believe* that those rules don't apply to us, and then we extend that for people we favor and not for anyone else, and *that* feels like crap.

When we convince ourselves that the rules don't apply to us, we end up usually doing really, really, *really* terrible things—or, if we're lucky, just slightly terrible.

It throws us out of integrity, and being out of integrity is one of the worst feelings for most intensives.

That has large-scale implications for our mental health, for our leadership, and for the health of our institutions.

3 – 12

THE PUSH

We have power. We *like* power. We carry a lot of power.

Not everyone does.

We have this thing as intensives: We want our dreams *now*. But sometimes it's not totally up to us. Sometimes we need the love and support or presence or muscle of someone else. This is where it gets tricky. We are *so clear* about the thing we want, and *so clear* about how it could happen, if only Miguel and Mary and Tanisha would get on *board* already. Dammit! But they are, totally reasonably, doing their own thing at their own pace, in their own way and time. And so here we are, chomping at the bit.

If we are not *totally* on top of our internal work, we will give in to temptation and start using our considerable personal power and motivation to try and nudge (and then shove) everyone into place. Then we start *pulling* people along as hard as we can, keeping their motivation in line with our vision.

This is leadership, but it's not sustainable leadership. It will wear you right out. Completely. Totally. Doesn't matter if you're a chef running a kitchen or a minister running a church or a principal running a school or a CEO running a startup, being the whole driving force behind your organization will kill you—probably sooner rather than later. It also has the insidious possibility of convincing you that your worth is somehow tied to the success or failure of your enterprise (hint: *wrong!*) and that as go you, so goes your crew. If you're *that* entwined, you're doing it wrong. You're also putting *way* too much pressure on yourself. So stop.

While it is tempting to push and pull so you never ever have to wander off the path you plotted, it is far healthier to allow for some meandering. You can set a course from A to B *knowing* (and setting deadlines as if) you're going to be spending time off course, sent there by the unexpected, the unpredictable, and the human—because it's not just you.

Learning to allow yourself and your project to wander can be tricky. Your vision will be clear and your focus will be intense. You, unlike your expansive teammates, have a limited window in which to at least lay the rough draft down, start to finish. If you don't reward your brain with the "I DID IT!" chemistry pretty soon, you'll drop it. So, as with family who are less intense than you are, set yourself a subset of tasks that you can work away on while the expansives in your life get to their parts on their schedules.

More important, though, you're *not* using your energy to motivate other people. There's a fine line between inspiring them (excellent) and dragging them (not your job).

3 – 13

THE UTILITY OF
DISTRACTION

Meanwhile, back at the ranch (or, what to do while everyone else is wondering what to do):

You will probably, most likely, if you are working with *anyone* else, need a side project. That might be related to the main project. (If so, lucky you.) It might even be a few steps ahead on the main project (extra bonus points!), or it might be something else entirely. This is how we end up splitting our otherwise super-focused attention. Some momentum is lost in the conversion but it keeps us from making everyone crazy, so that's worth something.

If you are an adult intensive without a hobby, something is wrong. Either you've been going through a major depression, trauma, or upheaval, or you've just finished your dissertation. You probably haven't *noticed* that the hobby is missing yet. It's a bigger problem than you think. Find one immediately. Take two—they start off small.

Ideally, your hobby should be something scalable, so you can expand or contract it to make it fit the space you have. My hobbies range from woodworking to knitting to music, and I've finally stopped beating myself up about dropping something for three or six or twelve years and then suddenly being ready to pick it up again. Lifestyle and the natural ebb and flow of an intensive brain mean that we don't always do the same thing, and that's okay.

If you can't remember what you like to do, ask yourself: What did you like as a child? If that's no help, pick five random activities to do over the next two weeks and see which appeal to you most. I never would have guessed, but it turns out I love surfing. And clothing design? I'm working on that, too—but of course it's to create a specific thing that I think should exist that doesn't, not a general design hobby. What do you do all the time in your spare time? Browse real estate listings? Fantasize about making amazing food? Pay attention—this is the stuff that you can do to keep your brain happy. And it could become your career.

My delightful editor Sarah Grey points out that hobbies also can help you concentrate or rebalance your system, such as doing a tactile activity after an ephemeral one, or doing puzzles while your subconscious needs to chew on something undisturbed.

Bottom line: You *need* to be mentally active. It's in your bones. If you're not, you will get seriously cranky. So keep yourself busy, engaged, and curious, and spend time with people who either make space for that or join you in it. It's awesome.

On the other hand, only write a book (or do any other long-form work) if you really have something to say or if the characters won't shut up. "How hard can it be?" is not for sideline projects, because you are likely to lose interest and drop it, and then you will feel weird about the loose end floating around out there. I love to write; it's one of my chosen arts, yet sitting down at the keyboard some days is really challenging. Once I start and get into a groove, it's fine—it's fun, even, it's exciting. But the inertia is pretty strong.

Also, if you *do* choose a long-form project, give yourself clear and consistent milestones so you can see your progress. Every time I sit down to write on one of my books, I have a word-count goal. It helps me keep moving and lets me know when I can reasonably stop.

This goes for bodies, brains, even institutions. If your organization is inherently intensive, nothing else will do.

3 – 14

INTENSIVE AND EXPANSIVE INSTITUTIONS

Institutions as well as individuals can be intensive or expansive. They have the same characteristics as individual people do, and when an institution is intensive it's really helpful—although not required—for the leadership team to match the character of the institution. That is, if the organization is intensive, having an intensive leader, or expansive with expansive.

Expansive institutions, like expansive individuals, like to take things slowly, in measured fashion. The culture of the institution itself is one of considered choices, carefully weighed. Impulsiveness is discouraged, and crises tend to throw the entire system for a loop unless there are specific and concrete step-by-step systems for dealing with them. Improvisation makes everyone uneasy. The people here are excellent at long-haul, sustained work, inside the building and out. This is an institution of small gifts and work done one day at a time. Too many changes overwhelm and exhaust the system and people disengage.

Intensive institutions, on the other hand, are risk-takers. They get excited by stretch goals and major transitions. They take to new initiatives like a duck to water. If there isn't enough variety in the life of the institution, people become distracted and productivity goes down.

The challenge with an intensive institution is that it is still probably populated with a mix of intensives and expansives, and the expansives *may* have a hard time with intensives' choices, beliefs, and behaviors.

Intensive clergy, for example, need a lot more leeway than expansive clergy. And an institution that can't give that to them shouldn't call them.

Why? Because the daily work of an organization involves a lot of usually-expansives (accountants, administrators, and so on) in key roles. They keep the organization running. But intensive clergy need to be able to function in an intensive way. They "just know" something will work and, unless it is going to bankrupt the organization, they probably need room to do it. Policy governance, which is very popular right now in nonprofits, was designed for an intensive leader and a mix of expansive and intensive board members. The board, rather than saying what the leader *does*, says what the leader may *not* do, and then the leader gets to do more or less whatever else they want. (But if they piss off the board, they get fired.)

Expansive get nervous around intensives. They see us as impetuous, unpredictable, brilliant-but. They don't see, can't imagine, the processing that goes on before we say, "Hey, let's buy all the buildings on the block!" (This is a real example). We can explain it six ways from Sunday, or we might not know ourselves exactly how we know that this is a good idea, but we *just know*.

There's no way for us to tell them that, fifty years later, we will use the space to create a resource, a building addition that the organization and the city desperately need. We don't actually *know* that. What we know is that there is potential and we can't allow the moment to pass.

Our ideas don't generally work well under compromise conditions. Buying just half the buildings might not work.

We tend to be charismatic leaders. The people who like us stay. The people who don't like us leave. They leave because they can't trust us, and we can't always explain ourselves well enough to win trust.

What we can convey is not mechanical details, which we may not have, but *vision*. And it's the fire in our bellies, the fierceness of our visions, the vastness of possibility, that draw the people who stay toward us.

Again, this is true of both the intensive institution and the intensive leader.

An intensive institution cannot survive more than a year or two of an expansive leader—it will lose the momentum and energy that make it run. An expansive institution will be uneasy with an intensive leader.

If the congregation or the institution has experienced trauma, then it's nearly always useful for the institution to go through a period where the leadership is more expansive than intensive. Trauma might be a crime or embezzlement, a CEO stepping down under questionable circumstances, or a near-bankruptcy. Trauma shakes not just the routine but the identity of the institution itself. Healing from trauma or major disruption happens better in an expansive environment, regardless of who you are. Conversely, when an expansive institution is transitioning between leaders, it can be helpful to have an intensive acting or interim leader lead the transition. Intensive congregations need expansives for about six months; then they need to go back to normal. Expansive congregations need expansives for about six months; then they need to be re-empowered, and that happens more easily with an intensive.

In a more traditional interim, the expansives in the rank and file can get shaken up a little bit—they can be offered some other ways to look at things, get a new perspective, have a little stress and a little growth, and then what happens is that stress fractures things just enough that when the institution comes together with its new expansive leader—the permanent leader—the expansive has cracks into which roots can grow.

In a lot of his teachings, Reid Mihalko, a sexuality and relationship coach and educator colleague of mine, uses the phrase "Date your species." What he means is that there are things you shouldn't fight. In the end, intensive organizations often have an easier time with intensives at the helm. Expansive organizations are more likely to relax and thrive when expansives lead.

If you choose a leader who is completely different from who you are as an institution, expect that to be an interim, a growth or healing time, or a relationship that requires consistent tending. It's not that crossing the line isn't possible, just that doing it well requires ongoing awareness.

3 – 15
CODESWITCHING

An intensive growing up in an expansive space learns really early to moderate, to mute, to adjust, to express themselves in such a way that their expansive environment will respond positively to them and will meet their needs. If you are an intensive kid in an expansive family, and in an expansive cultural space then you have to be expansive at home, at school, at work, on the playground—even though your natural expression is intensive.

Then, every so often, you run into intensive friends or colleagues—peers—and suddenly you can relax and you feel you can breathe; you can just be yourself. And until now you didn't know why you clicked so well with those people.

The answer turns out to be because your expansive environment has been removed for a while; you're immersed with intensives, and you are in a space that matches who you are.

Expansives have never had to do this unless they grew up in an intensive household—because the culture in which they find themselves outside the home favors expansives. Some families are going to have an intensive culture, like some institutions do, but most families here in North America have an expansive culture. So if you are mismatched with your family you had to adapt your behavior either way, but intensives have it a little harder because there's no escaping when you leave the house—you codeswitch all the time.

Codeswitching is a term borrowed from linguistics and then from African American and Deaf contexts of behavior; in those contexts, it describes switching between dialects and methods of communication as well as cultural patterns. I use it here to refer to switching between cultural patterns depending on the social context.

Intensives get good at codeswitching, like all minorities do. But when you reverse it—when you ask people in an expansive cultural matrix who are themselves expansives to start interacting better with intensives, asking *them* to codeswitch, you're asking them to learn how to function in an intensive environment as well as *you* function in an expansive environment. You think it's not really a big deal and they should just step up and *do* it—because you're used to doing it. *They are not used to doing it*, and it's a new skill. That's really important to know.

As an intensive, you have practice acting expansive because you have to do it to survive. As an expansive—a member of the dominant cultural paradigm—they may never have had to codeswitch. *Ever.*

(By the way, this happens anytime a member of a minority group asks a member of the dominant culture to code switch. Equality feels like oppression or an undue burden to them, because they have never had to do it and don't know how.)

I'm encouraging compassion here, which is not always our strong suit.

Asking an expansive to adapt to an intensive environment is like expecting someone with no experience to hop on a bicycle and ride the Tour de France. They can't even ride a bicycle. It's possible they've never even been on a tricycle. As a minority population, it is unfortunately incumbent on us, the intensives, to teach people until there are enough people in the majority out there who know that they can teach themselves. I wish this weren't the case, but we can either teach or die.

That's why I'm writing this book—because teaching people over and over and over again is exhausting for you, but it's something that you end up having to do. Part of the responsibility of being a minority in any population is that you have to help people bridge the gap, because they have no resources and no idea what they're doing. Every so often you run into an ally: You find an expansive who grew up in an intensive family or an expansive who works with intensives all day or an expansive who learned to be intensive in order to pursue the career they wanted to pursue, like emergency-room doctor or like chef. When you find those people? *Enlist their help!* Recognize that they are translators. Tell them that you need help. Hand them this book.

Codeswitching doesn't come naturally. It's a learned skill that minorities learn so young that we very rarely recognize that we even have it. We just assume that everybody can do this thing, and we don't even know that we're doing it, but in fact it's very nuanced and skilled—and not everybody can do it. Most of the expansives around us have never been challenged around their expansiveness. When they *are* challenged, sometimes they just figure they wandered into a place that's all wrong and they leave and don't have to be further challenged by it—because there's another way to get that need or that condition met.

A Third Note to Expansives: How (and Why) to Codeswitch

Dear expansives,

I know it's uncomfortable and hard. But the world needs you to learn to function intensively sometimes, because we need a mixed cultural space, not a cultural monolith. If you have learned, for example, that shouting means somebody is out of control and needs to wait until they're subdued, then it takes quite a bit of practice to see shouting as legitimate self-expression. But it is, and seeing and experiencing it without prejudice is key to creating a cultural world that has space for everyone. (I'm not talking about shouting *at you*, though. Abuse is different. Boundaries are important around that kind of situation. It's sometimes hard, especially if you have a trauma history, to see the difference at first.)

If you're an expansive and you're really struggling—if you get triggered, either because you grew up in a household where shouting was a sign of danger or one where nobody ever shouted—then you might have to learn how to talk about what you need in the moment, and that's really tricky. But you can't make it about the other person.

As an expansive in a heated conversation, if you raise your hand

and you say "I'm sorry, you're really out of control. Can you calm down before you talk?"—that's not going to help, because you're externalizing the problem. You're so used to having a cultural space that belongs to you, that caters to your needs and your expectations and your habits, that you think anybody who isn't catering to that is wrong. As the expansive, you're saying to the intensive, "There's something wrong with you. Fix the thing that's wrong with you so that I can be more comfortable." Instead, to make this work, it's actually expansives who have to shift. You, the expansive, have to own what you feel. Intensives really respond well to feelings, but they have to be *your* feelings.

So what do you do instead?

Experiment with discomfort, and notice that you get to *choose* whether you deal with discomfort like this or not. Try getting used to it instead of asking people to change, because that's the difference between being in the dominant cultural group and being in a minority cultural group.

Unless we shift the paradigm, the dominant cultural group gets to say "I'm uncomfortable so this has to change," but the minority cultural group can't say that, because they don't enough voices in the room to change it. This is true even if you have mostly intensives and just a couple of expansives in the room. Intensives have been conditioned for so long by so many people to believe that their behavior is actually the problem—to believe that their *way of being in the world* is actually the problem—that they will believe it. Even if there are only three expansives and ten intensives in the room, if an expansive says "Could you calm down?" intensives are likely to have a huge wave of shame and guilt and then to try to be more expansive to make the expansives more comfortable, because that's what we've been trained to do. *We need to stop doing that.* We are participating in our own silencing.

We need to not feel guilty for being ourselves, because that means no one gets to find out what we have to offer.

As intensives, we are instead asking the expansives to stop exercising their privilege and to start letting us set the tone and see that as legitimate. If everyone in the room is an intensive, the volume goes up and the energy goes up. The speed of speech goes up and everyone gets really animated and people feel like the other people in the room *care*. People feel engaged, and it can be absolutely amazing. Lisa Nichols, a dynamic coach and transformational speaker, does a conference every year that's packed with intensives. In fact, if you're an intensive entrepreneur looking for your people, look her up. It is a completely different experience.

Now, this can get to an extreme—people can come to blows. Intensives need the moderating effect of expansives sometimes, and we also need common sense. We don't want people to end up injured. That's not intensiveness or expansiveness. But it needs to be okay for the room to be big and loud, and expansives tend to react to that by shutting down and withdrawing and stopping participating in the conversation—and we need expansives not to do that. We need expansives to *stay with it*, to be present without being flattened. Expansives can choose to say, "Wow, everybody's really shouty and loud, that's really interesting." And it's totally reasonable to wait for the conversation to come to a pause and then raise your hand and say, "So have I got this right?" and lay out what you think has been said so that you can think about it as an expansive in an intensive space. You might need space or time; you might need to go find a closet to sit in while you think it over; you might need lots of things—and it's okay to meet your needs.

But it's *not* okay to impose on a roomful of intensives, and that's the hard part for someone shifting out of dominance. The hard part is learning that it's okay to meet your needs by changing *yourself*, finding ways to meet your needs on your own, and not expecting everyone around you to change in order for your needs to get met.

If you must ask for a change, assume that it is an imposition and only ask if it's a crisis.

Say what's true for you: "This reminds me of danger because..."

Say what you'd like: "Could you speak more quietly?"

Be prepared to meet your need by some other means if necessary (like quietly excusing yourself).

Use it sparingly. As an expansive, you're in the dominant population and you're used to the world being built for you.

A note about contexts where antiracism work is going on: It is rarely appropriate to ask people to change their behavior if you are a white person and the people of color are talking. "Tone policing," where you ask someone to change their self-expression style to make you more comfortable or judge them for the way in which they express themselves, is an old, embedded way of silencing minority populations.

When we all figure this out, we will be three steps closer to world peace.

It's really, really vital for all of us to understand these differences—not just the intercultural conflict-model differences, but the more subtle and nuanced ones, the gifts and challenges for each of us.

When expansives welcome intensiveness, things will change.

When expansives can deliberately say, "Oh, look, this is a situation where an intensive would be useful—John, you're an intensive, would you mind coming up and leading this section?";

When intensives can raise their hands and say, "I'm pretty sure what we need is an intensive lens on this";

When interrupting is seen as a cultural difference and not necessarily rude, and when staking space in a conversation by saying, "Hang on, let me finish my point," is seen as a cultural difference and not necessarily rude;

When intensiveness is seen as a strength and expansiveness is seen as a strength;

When leadership teams are deliberately chosen with an intensive and an expansive so that all the skills are covered;

When boards are chosen with a mix of intensive and expansive so that everything gets done;

When initiation tasks are handed off to intensives and sustenance tasks are handed off to expansives and there is a deliberate effort to give everybody involved the same amount of credit—

The world we live in is going to change.

Love,

Intensives

3 – 16
THE RIGHT PERSON
FOR THE JOB

This is about knowing there are different skill sets and using them. When you have a project that needs to be just dived into and dealt with, you send in an intensive; that's what we do well. When you have a project that you know can drag on for years and that has lots of little fiddly bits that are going to come up a little at a time, if you assign an intensive to that the project, it will fail. Assign an expansive, and have the support of an intensive.

When it is a particularly sensitive negotiation, you send in an expansive. When there is a negotiation that's all about staying raw and open, you send in an intensive. When you need to bond fast and you don't have any time to do it twice, you send in an intensive. When you need to build a long, longitudinal relationship a little at a time, you send in an expansive.

Get the intensives to help with the startup phase. Get the intensives to help with that one major push, get an intensive on board when everybody else is exhausted from working on a project for 80 or 90 percent of the way—bring in an intensive who hasn't been looking at the project, who sees it as a new project, and you get a burst of energy and focus to get it done and bring it to a big, beautiful finish.

This is about not making people wrong, or accusing people of not caring or being overly emotional; this is about recognizing the inherent worth and dignity in every person and making good use of the skills that they have. This is about understanding where use of the democratic process makes things harder; this is about understanding when a majority vote is not the appropriate decision-making tool; this is about understanding when the loudest voice in the room might not be the right decision-making force.

This is about understanding what people are good at and reducing the stress in the system by asking them to do the things they do best. This is about recognizing that *every single one* of these people—each of the expansives and each of the intensives—has a skill set that's needed.

This is about knowing when you just have to trust your leader and go with your eyes closed and your heart in your throat, and when you need to see a plan laid out end to end very clearly—and in each case, asking the right person to do the job.

Yes, if you're negotiating with a rival or somebody who does not have your best interests at heart, you need somebody who can fake it—who can pretend or who can at very least mask how they feel. There *are* intensives who can act—they might be the right person for that negotiation. But you don't want a truthful intensive in that situation—we are terrible at lying. We try periodically because we're human, but we're terrible at it and we should not be doing it, especially professionally. On the other hand, when you feel like there's a rift, when you feel like there's a gap and you need someone to go in and figure out how to connect, you need somebody who can say what they feel. Knowing what the other person is—expansive or intensive—will help you find someone who can match them.

It's really vital work to understand this in yourself—in your cultural context, your family, your work, your faith community—and it's really important to understand it in others. This is a tool for building connection; this is a tool for making space; this is a tool for breaking down what has been a dominant cultural paradigm and shifting the focus, so that people who have not been historically centered can be brought level with people who have.

When we equalize what we value and what we honor and we recognize the equal value of everyone's skill set, then the world changes; then our cultural spaces change.

Sometimes that means that we deliberately bring expansive intentions into an expansive leadership team; sometimes that means that we look at our style of doing business and we deliberately insert intensive elements. But we can't do that consistently unless we know what an expansive is, we know what an intensive is, we know who we are, and we can see it in the people around us.

As I said earlier, it will be easier if you have an expansive institution with an expansive leader and an intensive institution with an intensive leader. There are exceptions in times of stress or trauma recovery, but otherwise, that's the easiest way to go.

Now in the case of an institution like a church, which has several tiers of leadership, that leadership should be graduated from intensive to expansive, because even in an intensive congregation or institution, the institution will more or less reflect the ratio of intensives to expansives in the larger world.

Which is to say, in most situations an intensive institution will still have a 30 percent intensive to 70 percent expansive ratio. Because the institution is intensive, they will probably be closer to that 30 percent and not the 10 percent found in the dominant culture. (This figure is a guess, by the way. I'm hoping that someone takes this on as sociology or psychology research and confirms—or challenges—my estimate).

Moving up the rungs of leadership, that intensive institution will require a 50 percent intensive board and probably 100 percent or close to 100 percent intensive executive committee, plus an intensive leader.

Why is this important? The 30/70 happens automatically, just as a reflection of the world around us. In a deeply intensive institution it might be just a shade higher, but not much. You probably won't see even 40 percent, and 50 percent is highly unlikely in the United States and Canada, with very few exceptions. Expansive people accustomed to an expansive context are going to panic if they're constantly subjected to the level of intensity that the intensive leader puts out, even though they're in an intensive institution.

Most expansives—those who have normal or low tolerance for intensity—can't take that kind of intensity all the time, so those expansives stay out of leadership.

They keep their distance so they can function.

Imagine if the leader was always shouting. Expansives don't like to be in the room with that kind of volume. So rather than sitting in the same room as the shouting, which will make them climb the walls, they stay fifty feet away and then they don't get hurt by the shouting, and they can still benefit from what leaders think—they can hear it just fine from fifty feet away.

These are the folks who don't tend to move up in leadership in intensive institutions—at least not very much, and not very many of them. They may be excellent leaders in expansive spaces, but not intensive ones.

There is one very important group of exceptions, and they tend to be very successful. The expansives who *do* rise to leadership have a very high tolerance for intensives—maybe they grew up in a highly intensive environment, maybe they work in an intensive environment, but they had to become accustomed to having more intensity around them than your average expansive. They become really good leaders and important cultural translators in the institution. Those people should be on your board, in your executive committee, working as the intermediaries, serving as the filters between the intensity of the leader and that 70 percent of the institution who are expansives. So your executive board—the three or four people at the top and who are in very frequent consultation with the leader—need to be intensives. They're going to be in the presence of an intensive charismatic leader a lot, and if they find intensity uncomfortable or overwhelming they will probably hate it—and you never want your leaders to hate their jobs.

If you have somebody who hates being in that kind of intense environment, , put them somewhere else. They have talents you can use, but not there. Don't exhaust everyone by asking someone to do something that is outside their skillset.

3 – 17
THE SYSTEM IN ACTION

Let's take a look at how this balance might play out in practice through introducing an idea at a hypothetical nonprofit organization.

When the intensive leader has a wild idea, the leader presents it to the executive committee, whose members say, "That sounds like a great idea." Then they say, "Now let's strategize about how to bring it to the board."

They think about all the possible ways they could bring it to the board—all the ways they could present it, all the concerns the board might have—and they try to answer those concerns ahead of time.

The executive committee allows the leader to have a little moderation before they even go before the board (which is fifty/fifty intensives and expansives). The board listens and the intensives on the board probably say, "Good! When do we start?" …but the expansives on the board are probably going to have some resistance. That's a really common situation.

If you have intensives on the board who do not like the leader, they will probably push back really hard, and winning them over may well be harder than winning over the expansives.

The expansives are just nervous because it's all happening so fast and it's all so big. If you help them understand what the goal is, how you'll get there, and that you've considered all of their concerns, you can usually win them over.

On the other hand, an intensive who believes firmly that the leader is wrong is probably going to have to spend time with the leader to be convinced. If intensives don't care, then they are easy, but if they care and they're resisting, bringing them around can require a lot of time and attention.

If you have an intensive on the board who consistently doesn't see eye to eye with your leader, that's probably going make it really hard to get things done, but an intensive who agrees with your leader's general direction will get on board faster and be a fiercer advocate than most of the expansives in the room.

The expansives are going to need a little moderation, a little softening, a little convincing. That is part of what the executive committee does. As an intermediary, the executive committee figures out how to bring along the people who aren't quite ready. Expansives *want* to be ready; they want to agree, they want everyone to be at peace. They don't like conflict or high-intensity arguments, so if you can make it easy for them to get there, they'll come along. They have to feel like they are being taken care of and like nothing is moving too fast. They need to avoid panic, because when people panic then they put the brakes on.

So your executive committee needs to figure out how to give the expansives enough time and enough space to adjust. It takes time. Remember how expansives make friends slowly over a period of a year or two, so that they can have a really deep friendship? Expansives make friends with ideas, too, and this takes time in almost exactly the same way.

If you have an expansive institution and an expansive leader, the expansive leader takes their time and starts introducing the idea early and often. A couple of years in, if the institution is encouraged to move forward, the expansives in the institution will move forward easily.

But intensive leaders can have a complete vision that they want to execute as fast as possible, and if they don't act on their momentum it will be harder for them to move forward. They have to catch that wave while it's coming. The problem with that is that it means moving fast and expansives don't like that. If you can lay any groundwork, give the expansives a sense of where the leader might be going, or address their anticipated concerns, that's useful.

Expansives are the most likely ones to ghost. Intensives will storm out, but expansives will just drift away. They stop coming and don't tell anyone. The problem with that is that you can lose people over something that wasn't a problem at all. The solution to that is to have your board have enough expansives on it that the board can really get into the heads of the institution's members. The institution is 70 percent expansives; when the board gets into the heads of the membership—really thinks about how they feel, what they're really worried about, what will feel disruptive or uneven to them— then it becomes really easy for them to come up with a strategy for bringing a new idea to the institution in a way that will work for the expansives, and to stage the rollout in such way that it doesn't feel like it's coming all at once.

An expansive institution with an expansive leader will take its time. Intensives will tend to become very impatient in an expansive institution and probably should not be at very high levels of leadership. Intensives in an expansive institution can be put in charge of particular projects—things that are relatively untrammeled by the bureaucracy of the institution and that can be completed almost completely autonomously.

For example, intensives in an expansive congregation tend to lead things like social justice work, or community outreach, because you give somebody a specific social justice issue and tell them to find out about it and do it. It's independent work, they gather people around and get it done—they'll be happy as a clam. In a corporation, they might head a department like IT, where they are out of the usual promotion ladder and they make decisions as necessary without running plans through a lot of approvals. They just want to get it done, get out there, shout in the streets, write to the legislator, order the gear, whatever it is.

That's the ideal role for an intensive in an expansive institution. Intensives in expansive institutions are great for major projects; they're not great for interfacing with the membership around major projects. Let's suppose that there is going to be a building expansion. That's a huge project. Someone has to manage the political side of it—the publicity side of it—and if your institution is expansive, that should not be an intensive. Intensives in expansive institutions should pretty much never have the responsibility for speaking on behalf of the institution to the membership unless carefully supervised, because they will scare the expansives. But if you need somebody who will make sure that the architectural plans happen, do creative design from a pre-existing list of qualities generated, design work with the architect, push it through, make sure it happens—that's a great job for an intensive. Give them a job with an endpoint and clear parameters and then let them go.

This is very close to the Carver model of leadership—policy governance—which must have been created for intensive leaders working with boards and institutions. It's not really built for expansives—expansives don't need it to the same extent because expansives make decisions and do their work in a gradual, case-by-case, gentle, process-oriented way. It will probably still make life easier for an expansive leader, but it's not nearly as critical. Intensives do their work in a fast, somewhat judgmental, intuitive way.

The problem is that people who have concerns have no opportunity to voice them or they feel hurt or ignored, and that tends to fracture an institution.

Enter policy governance.

In this style of leadership, instead of having the leader come to the leadership team and say, "I have this idea," and have the leadership team debate it and figure it out and sort it out and make decisions and offer compromises (which won't work for an intensive), it allows for immediate action—within boundaries.

Intensives need to be able to act right away, without waiting for a committee meeting next month or for approval to come down through six levels of leadership, and they rarely can compromise their vision. Usually the vision does not work if it's compromised. Unfortunately, the best visions are often the most clearly all-or-nothing propositions.

So instead of decision by committee, here's what happens in policy governance: The board *sets limits* rather than approving everything. So our half-expansive board writes down two things: *what they're really scared of* and *what they really want.*

The transition to policy governance *forces* the board to figure out what they really want and what they're scared of. What they really want becomes the mission; what they're scared of become the limits. Out of that process there comes a document that says, "You can't do these things, because that's what we're scared of—it will destroy us if you drive us into bankruptcy, so you're not allowed to drive us into bankruptcy. You will destroy us if you completely change our leadership structure, so you're not allowed to do that." The board makes limits, but relatively few limits, and states them *really* clearly. Then the board says, "Here is our mission; your job is to actualize our mission in whatever way works for you." And then it lets go.

One of the hardest parts is that letting go, but that's the heart of the system. Once the board members let go, then an intensive leader can have wild ideas and do things that nobody else understands and make it work. The intensive gift is to think bigger than anybody else in the room is thinking, and then think ten times bigger than that, and *then* say, "Why not?"

3 – 18
Types of Organizations

There are, roughly speaking, three kinds of institutions:

- democratic or consensus-oriented organizations;

- authoritarian organizations that are pretty much independent; and

- authoritarian organizations that are hierarchical.

There is some correlation between intensiveness and authority—not 100 percent, but not zero. If you're really uncomfortable with authority, you are either an intensive in rebellion or you're an expansive who is expected to take authority that you don't want.

All of this is really important when we start choosing our leaders, so in the selection process it's important to know that there are some exceptions.

Let's step away from nonprofits and look at the tech industry.

Google appears to be an intensive institution—they like creativity, and (at least until recently) they set aside a chunk of everyone's work week for employees to do something innovative and creative.

They like change, they pivot fast, they don't give customers a lot of warning when they're about to change something. They rely on us to be resilient, iterative, and forgiving.

By contrast, Apple probably started out as an intensive institution, but it's not intensive anymore. If you look at the that they write and administer their software, it tends to be very authoritarian and very hierarchical; they tend to like things to be *just so*. They don't like chaos. They like creativity, but *only* in the development department. This has created fantastic branding and a really powerful sense of safety for customers, but everything is locked down.

People love Apple because it makes them feel safe and beautiful; people love Google because it makes them feel adventurous.

You don't really hang out with Google if you want safety. And you don't really hang out with Apple if you want adventure. That's okay—these two personalities draw two different crowds. The one exception is that Apple has a long-standing relationship with artists, and artists tend to be intensive. So even though Apple is no longer an intensive institution, they have some heritage of intensity that shines through.

Richard Branson of the Virgin group, whom I follow very closely, has been known to say there's a difference between an entrepreneur and an owner: Entrepreneurs start companies and they start them and they start them. Steve Jobs, on the other hand, started Apple and then stuck with it. He continued to manage it even after it was established. For entrepreneurs, the juice is in the establishment phase, in the startup phase. Once it's been started up, it's not interesting—it's going in a straight line at a constant speed unless the force is applied to it. It's fine.

Fine is fabulous. For expansives.

Excellent managers and excellent entrepreneurs are different groups of people. Where the excellent manager is consistent, predictable, and evenhanded, the excellent entrepreneur is a little off-the-wall, little higher risk, maybe even a little crazy. But that's okay. The beauty is that is it maps into our leadership.

The founder of the company is almost always an intensive, because you cannot found a company without an intensive. If you're an expansive founder, you probably brought an intensive on board first thing. Once you're up and running, once you have staff and assistants and you're clipping along at an even rate, that's when the entire character of the work shifts. That's the decision point: you have to figure out if, as a long-range identity, your institution is intensive or expansive.

If your institution is expansive, if it likes things consistent, if your customers like things consistent, if they like it to *just work*, then you are already expansive. Your company culture can reflect that.

If you decide you're an intensive institution, that doesn't mean you can't be stable. Google is stable. The whole Google brand is built around an intensive identity—that the people there are creative and innovative and come up with wild ideas and take information from everywhere they can get it and integrate it into the products that they create, and that they serve as many people as possible with these wild ideas. That's what being an intensive company looks like.

If you're an intensive company, then you can keep having an intensive CEO. In fact, your founder may be able to stay on at least for a while, which is not usually the case in expansive companies. Your intensive CEO will support that intensive culture, and you will probably end up hiring a high percentage of intensives, even well over 50 percent. Those intensives going to hire intensives to work under them, and that company culture continues to grow and spread. You can end up with a robust institution built on the experience and principles of intensiveness.

Highly authoritarian and *independent* structures tend to have intensive leaders, because they can function in an intensive way. Highly consensus-oriented organizational cultures tend to have a lot of expansive leaders because slow-and-steady *works* with democracy and consensus. Highly authoritarian and *hierarchical* institutions tend to attract expansives, or intensives with a high obedience factor.

One of the clearest places this appears is in churches.

In mainline Christianity, the independent Pentecostal church would be an example of a highly authoritarian and independent culture, the Quakers (Society of Friends) a highly consensus-oriented culture, and the Catholic Church a highly authoritarian and hierarchical culture.

As noted earlier, intensives with a high obedience factor become rigid in an unmalleable system. This can lead to abuses of one kind or another as they try to express their intensiveness within the structure of the organization. Expansives are a much better fit for these organizations. Even when they reach the top of the hierarchy, intensives are likely to suddenly make enemies as they make the radical changes they have been wishing would happen for the last four decades—Pope Francis is a good example. They are great for radical transformation, but they tend to get crucified afterward.

And yes, I *do* think Jesus was an intensive.

The Unitarian Universalist Association—a liberal religious denomination composed of independent congregations linked by a covenant and common governance—is an interesting case. I grew up and was ordained to UU ministry, so I've got an inside look at the institution. Like many congregationally oriented church organizations, we have both expansive and intensives congregations. We are a loose hierarchy. Individual congregations have a lot of autonomy, but we are not by nature very authoritarian. It has both helped us and hamstrung us.

Some of our churches, mostly the big city ones with downtown buildings, are meant to be intensive congregations. They have it in their bones, from back when intensives just about ran the church (as long as they were diplomatic white men).

The founding character of a church matters tremendously. For more on this, consider reading *Generation to Generation*, by Edwin H. Friedman and Gary Emanuel, about how family systems play out in churches. Those big stone edifices on main street require big energy, big vision, and leadership that borders on brash. That is who they were cut out to be.

The challenge is that when ministers get comfortable, they often start making choices for stability rather than for growth. They start getting attached to *staying* instead of attached to vibrant congregational life.

On the other hand, introduce too much risk and half the congregation walks. The large congregation can tolerate a lot of expansives in an intensive group, because the expansives don't get so close to the leader that they can feel the ups and downs of everyday leadership. The executive committee should be mostly intensives, with maybe one expansive. The board should be a mix, fifty/fifty or so, higher than average. The lay leaders buffer the intensiveness for the expansives who just want to come to church on Sunday and have a place to bring their kids.

In a larger city, a choice of churches are best, two per denomination if you can manage it: one intensive, one expansive. People who find one to be a bad fit will seek refuge in the other. Sometimes the old church is expansive, as it has been from the beginning. This is often the case in small New England towns. In that case the radical, intensive church will start when someone gets frustrated with the slow process of the original church and storms out (or maybe it was over abolition, or theological differences). The rebel church must be careful not to lock itself into an identity of resistance, because if they grow, they will eventually be the authority they believe they must resist, and then they will dismantle themselves in order to maintain their own identity—or simply cycle between growth and chaos. Better to hitch that identity to intensiveness, and go ahead and be intense—and send people who find it too much to the church across town.

This also appears in businesses. Consider a small, scrappy startup. This business is bootstrapped by the founder's credit cards, and she ignores everyone who says it can't be done. When she starts to get traction, she hires an assistant and a geek-of-all-trades, neither of whom is local. They stay up all night solving problems on three coasts and in three time zones. They carry their phones everywhere, and none of them has a lover. Every time someone says something is impossible, she emails a challenge to her team and they all drop everything to work on it. Their first client is tiny; their next client is a multinational corporation. They say yes even though they have no idea how they are going to build capacity that fast.

They pull it off—and in six months, they are the industry go-to.

Even as that company grows, it is likely to retain the qualities of intensiveness if no one makes a deliberate choice not to do so.

Compare that to a carefully orchestrated, well-established startup: The company gets funded by several well-regarded funders, there is a business plan, there is a hiring plan, everyone comes into the office every day. That's an expansive way to start a company, and that company will probably stay expansive as it grows.

A company can make a concerted effort to change, especially when the CEO changes (usually when the founder steps aside). The most common choice is to switch from intensive to expansive. If that happens well, often the original staff will ease out; you can make that work better by offering them a golden handshake. They will know intuitively that the company is going in a direction that doesn't fit—help them leave with grace.

It is by accepting who we are that we can do the best work we have available. Sometimes we change, we switch, we shift. But sometimes we just have to find that the thing we use to define ourselves has been a side characteristic, and when we find the central identifier, we become coherent and everything flows.

PART FOUR

THE CARE
AND FEEDING
OF YOUR
INTENSIVE
BRAIN

4 – 1
MENTAL HEALTH AND THE DARK SIDE

I'm about to take you to the uncertain, tricky, and utterly critical world of mental health and addictions.

This, very briefly, is my story about those things:

I lived with depression until I was almost forty, coupled with anxiety and trauma. The history of that is not particularly important here, but it goes deep into my childhood. The important part is that I survived the depression and found a treatment protocol that put it into remission. My capacity is dramatically increased as a result of it. Because my body is very sensitive to any attempts to mess with its chemistry, I found solutions that were minimally chemically invasive. Everyone is different. I've been in remission for a year as of this writing and it has completely changed my life.

As a result of the remission, I'm setting much better boundaries. I'm spending less time with abusive and addicted people. I'm spending way more time with people I like, and it's not nearly as dangerous for me to spend time by myself if there's no one I like available.

Also as a result of the remission, I'm able to do work that comes from my heart, which was much harder to do with depression. I'm able to write this book.

The world needs us, even if we're hurting or damaged or a bloody mess. The world needs our gifts, even if we have no idea what they are or who they help or when or how.

There's a tricky line here. It would be morally and factually wrong to say that we need to be healthy to give our gifts, because that's not true.

But I can say that it's a hell of a lot easier to live life without depression breathing down my neck and burning my spirit to ash every seven to ten days.

You don't deserve to hurt. So this is what I know about intensiveness, mental health, and getting out of the mess.

Onward.

Up From the Bottom of the Well
(originally published on my blog)

Usually, I'm pretty upbeat. I like to dwell in the sweet, the erotic, the pleasures, the finer things in life. I like to focus on the good stuff and help it get bigger.

But there's a danger in focusing **only** on the good stuff. It makes it hard to figure out how to get there. If you don't talk about the hard, well, it's almost impossible to build a bridge without two pieces of land to connect. Focusing on where you're going can be inspiring, motivating, and exciting, but it's not enough.

So let's talk about depression. Here in Maine, as I write this, we've stepped into Real Winter, with snow that sticks, cold days, colder nights; sunrise is after seven, sunset is before five. There are things I love about it: the crisp air, the unspeakably bright sun (when it's up), the crystalline sky. But come a cloudy day and it feels like the world has had the air sucked right out of it. There are all kinds of reasons why people get depression: body chemistry, circumstances, lack of sunlight, but it all boils down to one thing: *You feel like you're sitting at the bottom of a very deep well, and you don't even have the strength to stand.*

Breathing is hard. Not crying is hard. Moving is hard. Caring about anything, having hope for anything, is damn near impossible.

And pleasure? Food? Sex? Forget about it.

Maybe you're one of those people who eats to feel better. Or maybe you've discovered that you can drown your sorrows in the Internet or in chemicals of one kind or another. Or maybe you don't know any of that about yourself yet, or maybe you're too tired to try.

I lived with depression for my first twenty-four years. In 2001 I started to get a glimpse over the edge of the well. A few years ago, I finally climbed out. It's a slippery bank. I fall in again sometimes. And if you're completely exhausted, it's so tempting to just let go.

But as writer and designer Bridget Pilloud writes, we've gotta get moving. We've got to climb out. We have to. It's about survival. It's also about the amazingness of the world. And about not letting the bastards get you down. And about one more sunrise or baby smile—whatever your thing is, that thing that you bring to the world. But when you're way down there, down so deep in the shaft that you can barely see daylight, barely even remember it, let's be real: You don't give a damn.

So here's my personal step-by-step, the hidden ladder anchored in those cold, slippery stones. Of course, your needs and results may be different.

1. Totally contrary to every holistic piece of advice out there, sleep with your phone and your computer, or whatever you use to be connected to people who care. If you have no one who cares, whatever you use to be connected to the world outside your bed.

2. If you are not sleeping, don't lie in bed. Get up, give in, be awake. Write the crazy things in your head (on a notepad, where you can't impulsively email them out).

3. Have a therapist. Bring your notebook.

4. if you are sleeping, and especially if getting up is a challenge, create routines. Make deals: I just have to do these three small things and then I can go back to bed if I want.

5. Brush your teeth and your hair every day; shower at least once every other day. Change your clothes. You know how good it feels when you've got a cold and you finally get clean again? You are sick—like having the flu—and you'll feel worse if you let your personal hygiene go.

6. Give yourself gold stars. Don't roll your eyes. I'm serious. On a good day (or get a friend to do it for you) go shopping. Get a package of those tiny foil stars that your teacher handed out in third grade (if third grade was in the eighties) and a regular wall calendar. Staples has 'em. Every time you get up? Gold star. Brush your teeth? Green star. Journaling because it makes

you feel better? Red star. Asking for help? A whole line of silver stars (I know how hard it is to ask). It's easy to believe you Haven't Done Anything At All. Which is total bullshit. Your depression has a megaphone and it's shouting right in your ear. The stars help you find reality again.

7. Drink lots of water. I know, again with the rolling of the eyes. There are several reasons why this works. The big one is this: Stress and depression create toxins in your body. Water helps your body get rid of the toxins, like flushing the toilet. Start with a big glass, preferably with lemon, every single day. Then carry it around with you. Another bonus: if you tend to eat absently, substitute drinking water instead and you'll be less likely to gain random weight from not paying attention and more likely to feel full.

8. Make at least one phone call every day to someone outside your bubble of depression. They will change the endless loop in your head.

9. Do something with your body: Walk, cook, paint, dance, do yoga. Do not just sit still sixteen hours a day.

10. Give yourself an outlet: Journal, scream, cry. Give yourself some time every day to engage with whatever is awful. It feeds on sideways glances and the crap it finds under the rug when you sweep it there.

11. Get touch. I cannot emphasize this enough. Oxytocin would be reason enough, but there's more than that. Get someone to hold you; get a massage; if all else fails, take a bath or shower just to feel your skin again. Depression causes intense disconnection. Touch is one of the most basic ways to return to your body, even

just for a few minutes.

12. Take the pressure off. Tell the grumbling voices in your head that they are nothing but a pack of cards (as Alice in Alice in Wonderland would have it), and remind yourself that you are ill, you have come down with the mental equivalent of a fever, and you simply won't be functioning at full force for a while. Celebrate the little stuff and be realistic about what you can actually expect to do. If you can't be realistic, get someone who understands depression to help you set goals. This can be a friend, co-worker, coach, doctor, therapist... but not someone who is always totally cheerful and runs a marathon before breakfast.

13. Ask for help. I know. This might seem impossible. Still. Sign up for Mark Silver's remembrance challenge, which automatically calls you to do a little heart-centering every day for two weeks. Get a friend to promise to call you every other day just to talk. Tweet a call for funniest websites of the day. You don't have to bleed all over everyone to get assistance; you don't have to humiliate yourself or bare your soul. Just ask for a little help with something you need. Groceries. Laughter. Company. A kitten.

14. Pet a cat. Or a dog. Or a hamster. Don't have one? No problem, visit a friend, offer to pet-sit, or go visit a local pet store. Touch. Pleasure. Unconditional love. It doesn't get much more healing than that.

15. Help someone out. Sometimes the best cure is to stop thinking about it and lend a hand. Give someone a ride or a place to sleep or a book recommendation.

16. Do something you're great at. It's hard to tell from the

depths of depression, but there's probably still something you can rock. Find it. Do it. Set yourself up for success. Know how to knit? Make a potholder or a pair of fingerless mitts. Know how to read? Make a recording of fifteen poems for a friend who has a long commute. Bonus: These make great gifts.

17. Make your list of ten things. People don't like to say it, but depression can lead to thoughts of suicide. So make your list of ten (healthy) things you can do instead of killing yourself. Post it somewhere easy to see. You don't have to wait until you're that bad to use the list. Whenever you're at a loss, pick something and do it. The more you do, the more likely you are to shake the depression.

18. Escape. Sometimes, you just need some relief. It's like any pain: The pain causes tension, which causes more pain. If you can't relieve the tension, sometimes you can break the cycle with some temporary pain relief. I don't at all recommend alcohol or drugs for this. But a favorite TV show, a novel, or a couple of hours to do nothing productive on the Internet could be just the ticket.

19. Listen to music. For reasons that we don't totally understand yet, music touches our brains in ways that other things don't. Art does, too. Go to a museum or a concert, put on an playlist, and lose yourself in the art.

20. Breathe. When your brain gets scrunched, your breathing does, too. You need air and spaciousness in your chest so you can have air and spaciousness in your life. Spend a minute or two focusing on filling your chest with air and letting it out again.

21. Call yourself good things. Sweetie. Darlin'. Love. Words like stupid, no good, failure, and useless really aren't useful, especially if you're addressing yourself. Especially avoid words like lazy, which conflate your behavior (doing less) with a judgment (should be doing more).

The trick with depression is to do one small, tiny, manageable thing at a time. Overwhelm is easy to find. Don't go looking. Recovery is a series of tiny steps forward, without beating yourself up for backsliding. Do one little thing every day. And if it gets really bad, call a hotline. 1-800-273-TALK will work in the United States.

It's a tough time of year for a lot of people. Go gentle.

4 − 2
SQUISHED AND FRIED:
NOT RECOMMENDED

When you're told all your life that you shouldn't do something, sometimes you get lucky and you resist.

But *sometimes* you listen.

And if you listen too long and too well, it becomes so embedded in you that you think it *is* you.

It isn't.

Then you get inexplicably grumpy at people who can be that thing that you are, that thing you've been squishing for so long.

And you get overly righteous about people following the Rules, the ones that you're following, the ones that keep you squished.

This can happen to intensives, as I noted earlier in this book. We get squished.

This can also happen to expansives. Expansives get fried.

Expansives burn out trying to be intense.

Intensives get compressed into staying calm and level. Intensives are not, by personality, calm and level.

When we try to do something we're not built for, for too long, under stress…

We get sick.

When we get squished, we start to deteriorate. We lose our grace, then our calm, then our equanimity, then our pleasure in life. We can eventually get depressed or severely anxious (and by *eventually* I mean by the time we're four, or not until we're adults—either one.)

That's painful and damaging and challenging, but we are the primary victims.

Until we aren't. Not only does this affect our families and loved ones and colleagues, but sometimes we can take our intensiveness to a really bad place where we do the greatest damage to those around us.

I mean, that's true anywhere for anyone, but really, this one is tricky. All the evil and despotic world villains we talk about as who *not* to be? Probably, most likely, intensives.

Being an intensive is a delightful thing. Until you're teetering on the edge of destruction. As with most destructive tendencies, if we don't admit it, that's when it's most dangerous.

The real question, though, is this: what makes it happen? What takes a sweet child with an intense personality and turns them into a terror?

That's not unique to intensives. But we seem to have the greatest incidence.

Rejection. When we are rejected or feel rejected (whether we are actually being rejected or not), we start to feel misunderstood. We feel alone, but more importantly, we feel like our very *being* is wrong. When that takes root, we have two choices. Either we go deep into depression, or we reject all external feedback and decide the person rejecting us doesn't know what they're talking about.

That sometimes leads to...

Entitlement. We feel like everyone should understand how brilliant we are, and if they did then the world would fall at our feet.

Fear. This includes fear of being hurt, fear of being alone, fear of being rejected, fear of failure.

Anger. At rejection, at feeling overly unique, at not being recognized, at feeling afraid all the time.

And most of all: *Isolation.*

Surround anyone with loving support and modeling and you at least improve the chances that their spirit will take the hint, but this is especially true for intensives.

We are, often, people who want to heal the world. We think (rightly or wrongly) that we are special. And we are attracted to power, either unvarnished or in the form of sex.

If we get the idea that we can fix the world by killing a bunch of people, that's trouble. Because we have the force of will and charisma to make it happen.

You can't stop an intensive from being intense. You can't stop us from wanting to fix the world. You can only teach us by what means we might do that well.

Training ourselves to be loving is a perpetual process. If you give us love, or sex, or animal rescue, or hard work, or hiking, or dance—it doesn't matter what you put in our hands, we will use it to try to change the world.

What if Hitler had gotten into art school? We'll never know. Maybe he would have improved the lot of the German people through art.

It *is* important that we not condemn each other, and especially that we not condemn ourselves. We need to learn grace and forgiveness, starting with ourselves and our own mistakes, as early as possible. Early lessons in disappointment and internal castigation become later lessons in how to judge those around us, and those are toxic.

Judgment is not pretty. It leaves us trying to make sense of the world by deciding whether people around us are right or wrong. And that framework makes building relationship much harder, because we enter with an answer instead of with curiosity.

The impulse to get the world to conform to our standards is so strong that we might end up violating all our other principles in the process. That will leave us feeling angry and sad and out of alignment, and probably isolated from the people we are trying to control.

So often we find that we know intuitively things that others only realize later; that leads us to mistrust others in favor of ourselves, and *that* leads us to thinking that we know better.

Sometimes we do. Sometimes we don't.

Learning when to cede is as important a learning when to step up. Our job is to step up when it's needed. But not all the time, and not at the cost of love or lives.

We are here to make things better—to grow, to plant, to seed.

We must surround ourselves with people who will help us remember all the good things about the world, because otherwise it's too easy to see the parts that are damaged and fractured and struggling and too easy to decide that the only way to do it right is to start over.

And that's not our job.

We are not gods.

We are humans, with some power and some skills.

This is a world worth saving.

Don't ever tell yourself that you just have to live with being miserable. That's a lie the disease tells.

Get help.

Perspective helps. Support helps. Community helps. And using our power for good (and not evil) definitely, absolutely helps. It's a recursive cycle. The more we direct our intensiveness toward things that improve the world, the better it gets. The more we focus on the horrors, the more they consume us. Sometimes we find a way to numb ourselves, and sometimes a break is a good thing. But not too much, and not too long—moderation is *not* one of our native skills.

I discovered video games just about the time my family got a used Apple 2e from a friend. It was the era of *Frogger*, and I discovered that with enough persistence I could in fact get the little frog across the road with some consistency.

So I did.

In a world of complete chaos where cause and effect bore almost no relationship to each other, I could get the frog across the road over and over again. There was something to be said for that.

But the problem was that I felt like I had to get it right. Whatever "right" was. No matter how long it took. Success was addictive, and I craved success.

Sometimes I tend to talk about intensiveness as though it's all advantage, because the world around us is so bent on telling us that we're wrong for having it. However, telling only that side of the story would be as much a lie as pretending we didn't exist at all.

The truth is that we can get dark and scary in unknown ways and in unlit corners, and we can get bright white and scary, too. The Ku Klux Klan, Hitler, Machiavelli, those are all intensive people and places, too. This is not a one-sided Klein bottle.

I love being intensive—but it can kill you.

Not just in the literal sense of taking depression to the logical and fatal extreme, but also in the slightly less literal sense of encouraging us to heights of risk that are in fact dangerous. In every sport there are things you can do that will increase your risk. We can take risks and lose our jobs. We can push the edges and lose our relationships. We can decide that we want to take anything to an extreme that ultimately means we lose it and other things that matter to us.

We love risk, and that's great.

We hate losing, and that's useful.

But we have to be careful.

We're useless if we're dead.

This doesn't mean we should stop being intensives. Not that we could—that's like asking us to stop breathing. People try that all the time. That's why this book is here: because when people ask us to stop breathing, we suffocate. What it *does* mean is that we have to be aware of the times when it will be structurally or strategically a better choice *not* to follow our impulses. That's not nearly as frequently as most of the expansives around us would like us to believe. But it's still a number greater than zeo.

How do we know?

First and most immediate, we have an adrenaline threshold. You probably know the difference, the feeling in your body. There's a feeling that's excitement and then there's a feeling that's excitement tinged with dread. Dread is one of your most useful feelings. When dread shows up, *you should listen.*

We also have (or should have) a variety of friends around us with a variety of responses to our crazy ideas. Of those people, there are probably one or two who are absolutely, exquisitely good judges of bad ideas—at least when it's not *their* idea. Those people are your trusted advisors. They're probably intensives or understanding, middle-of-the-road expansives. They probably love you, and they are probably plainspoken. They will tell you when you're out of your mind. *You should listen to them.* If you don't have a couple of people like that, you can also pay attention to the average of the responses you get. The further from acceptance the average gets, the more likely it is that you should take a second look. Often people don't agree with us, but often there's some truth to their questions.

The other time intensive thinking can be a real liability is if you start thinking about negative or destructive things. Ex-partners are the classic example, but there's a whole raft of potential topics we try to fix retroactively. It's obsession, but more than that, it's obsession about things that are *bad for you to think about.* You could, for example, obsess about pears and no one would get hurt. But when you obsess about the test you failed in third grade or the ex-partner you can't help wondering about...

You cannot fix the past.

This is a vital lesson to learn. You. Cannot. Fix. The. Past.

You can apologize. You can make amends. You *can't* actually undo it. So stop thinking about it.

Most of the time, whatever the issue in question is, it's not even about you. People will tell you it is about you, or they won't. You'll be tempted to think it is about you anyway, and you'll spend time wondering what you could have done differently.

Don't waste your energy. After the first couple of weeks of over-analysis, get yourself a good, healthy distraction and put that shit down. If there was anything useful to discover, you'd have discovered it by day nine. If you did discover something, ask a friend, just to make sure it isn't horseshit. The,n if there's something to do, do it. If there isn't anything, get your healing process underway. Scream, shout, swim, hike, make art, take up a new language, start school—whatever your thing, *do* it.

Here's where the two sides of the intensive coin come in. On the one hand, you can be head over heels in love with your new project or idea. On the other hand, you can be completely absorbed by your grief. Allow some time to be sad, but put a timer on it. Get a friend to help you if you can't do it yourself. Take X years (if you really need years) to be sad, or X weeks or X days, and then you're going to get your ass out of your chair and do something useful. Onetwothreego.

Use your intensiveness to shift gears. Take on something big and brand new.

This is not to say you should not do your work, if you have work to do. If you have grief or depression or childhood trauma or anger issues, for God's sake, find a therapist you can trust (use your intensive qualities to make sure they're good, then nail your ass to their couch) and trust them. It will pay dividends for decades. Dive into the work.

But if there's something out of your control and you've already processed the hell out of it, find something else to immerse yourself in. Seriously.

4 – 3

RECONDITIONING THE BRAIN

So you've figured out that you're addicted to stress and you don't want to be. *Yay!* Knowing and battles and all that.

So.

How do you fix it?

First, get *really clear* that you're done with stress. That's absolutely critical. You, especially, as an intensive, need to be committed to change or nothing will happen. Clear out as much of the cobwebby but-maybe-it-helps-me-be-a-good-person or maybe-it-helps-me-get-things-done as you can. I know that stress isn't something you can just say, "sure, I'll get rid of that!" and ditch it, but you have to be ready to make some kind of major change.

Next: If your brain is already in a rut, here are a few tools that I've found helpful for getting out of it.

> 1. Belief repatterning. Suze Casey's book Belief Repatterning is an excellent guide, she also does one-on-one work and has a podcast. She

offers a step-by-step script that can be modified for a number of different situations in which you name and acknowledge the story you're telling that's got you stuck, then rewrite the story. Her specific language for the process is particularly effective.

2. Hypnosis is often useful for bypassing established habits of thought and function. There are some common misconceptions. For one thing, you're always in control of your own decisions, both in and out of trance. Your hypnotist is not only ethically bound to adhere to the agreed-upon treatments but is also unable to override your free will. Hypnosis just makes it easier for you to overcome your resistance by minimizing that resistance. You will not be made to do foolish things, and it's normal to remember everything that happens in a session unless you agree otherwise. I was very skeptical until I tried it, but it turns out to be a great way to talk with the subconscious—and it's also a great way to relax. It taps the ability of your subconscious to sidestep a lot of your usual patterns of thought, and you end up able to rewire your thinking very rapidly.

3. Exercise that requires your full attention, but isn't going to kill you if you mess up. Rock climbing with a good partner at a gym is a good example. Running is not. (Too much time to think.)

4. A good creative project. This gets your creativity hormones flowing, which feels good.

5. Martial arts, but not meditation. Meditation
    is a fine thing to try as a stopgap, but many
    intensives find that meditation just makes
    the obsessing worse. It's got too much time to
    think. You need something that takes all your
    attention. Martial arts, especially ones like tai
    chi and aikido, require a kind of deep focus
    that allows the brain to heal and rewire.

6. Ecstatic dance, sometimes.

7. If your brain/body are tending toward panic,
    talk to your therapist about bilateral stimu-
    lation. This could be vibrations, sound, or
    light that alternately appears on your right
    and left sides. The brain can't attend to that
    and maintain its panic/anxiety mode, so it
    has to put down the panic. This completely
    changed my anxiety response. Trauma ther-
    apists use a set of bilateral stimulation tech-
    niques called Eye Movement Desensitization
    and Reprocessing, or EMDR, but you don't
    need the EMDR protocols for bilateral stim-
    ulation to be useful. I used a Theratapper
    without EMDR, but a number of different
    kinds of bilateral stimulation may be useful,
    with or without EMDR protocols and direct
    supervision.

8. Binaural meditations work a bit differently,
    using bilateral stimulation of a different kind
    combined with gentle techniques related to
    hypnosis. The work of Paul Scheele (learn-
    ingstrategies.com) is excellent, as are the
    meditations by my dear friend Andy Dolph
    (binauraljourneys.com). They can be incred-
    ibly relaxing and restful, as well as helpful in

creating new patterns of thought.

9. Human touch is incredibly healing. If you have friends or a partner you can cuddle with, this is an A-plus strategy; nonsexual naked cuddling is the best. If not, massage is not the same, but it's better than nothing. If you like hugs, twenty seconds or more of a hug will allow your body to release some hormones (oxytocin, specifically) that will probably help.

10. Remove as much stress as you can from your life and get support in not creating more. I cannot emphasize this enough. Stress sends your body into fight/flight/freeze mode, which creates a biological and hormonal cocktail that's damn near impossible to fight your way out of. The first time in my life that I had to break this, I was hospitalized. I'm not kidding. This is serious, and seriously important.

Some combination of these will turn out to be good for you. For me, it took about six weeks to really complete the shift. These strategies allowed me to step down from the constant state of emotional (not sexual) arousal into a deep calm.

Since it's hard to remember these when your brain is being a pain in the ass, keep a written list taped to your wall if you need to (really).

Also, know your patterns. People of all genders have hormonal cycles, and they often follow a semi-predictable pattern. Learn what the signs are that this is just a crappy day, and be nice and gentle to yourself. Your day will come around.

Finally, do not forget your friends. Make sure you're seeing them, spending time enjoying them, and not shutting yourself away. It's important.

Here's how we get better: we don't.

Or rather, we do, but not the way people expect.

People tell us that we need to tone it down, back off, be different. People tell us that it is our job to make them comfortable. People seem to think that it's reasonable to think that we would just accommodate their lack of capacity or imagination.

It's not true.

Or, rather, not *often* true.

There are times: sick people, people planning a wedding, kids. Those are the times you'd just do it anyway, because the person you're accommodating needs a break.

But there are also times when we're so used to turning the volume down that we do it reflexively, but it feels terrible.

We're conditioned to ignore the feeling in our guts, but that feeling, the sense of this-is-right, the good-touch/bad-touch meter, is the most basic human direction-finder anyone has.

Even diehard, pure expansives have it, and if they can use it, it can make all the difference. But because we intensives set our sights so far in the future, the direction we pick matters a lot more. If you're sailing and your course is a few degrees off but you're going to the other side of the harbor, it's not terrible. If you're going to the other side of the world, you'll end up in a different country. We tend to aim for the other side of the world. Sailing across the ocean without navigational aids can kill you.

We are wired for risk, most of us, so we might take the chance—but really, that compass is a good idea.

Your body tries to tell you what it thinks, all the time. Most of us in the West have been largely trained to ignore it. We push through, we soldier on, no pain no gain, go go go. And we end up in bad careers, bad relationships, injured, sick, unhealthy, sad.

If you can't feel the direction you need in your gut:

Sit down and get really quiet. Close your eyes. Go from your toes to your head and just notice how each part of you feels.

Then focus specifically on your belly and abdomen. The part of your body most likely to send this kind of information is between your belly button and your knees. Allow all the feelings. Sometimes you'll feel turned on when you pay attention to the organs between your hipbones, your genitals, and your gut. Sometimes you'll feel yucky. It can open up a lot of old feelings as well as some new ones. Just let them come, ride them through, appreciate that you are getting all this information from your body.

Then notice other places. Notice the back of your neck. Notice your shoulders, your pectoral muscles, the tissues surrounding and protecting your heart, the outside edge of your hips, your low back, your thighs.

All the things you feel are information. Occasionally they are just information about your physical well-being (you tripped and stubbed your toe, now it hurts), but often the random sensations are not random at all. They are the keys to understanding your body's wisdom.

We don't know when we love someone; we don't know when we need to quit our jobs, *we don't know*. When we were all farmers and hunters, this knowing was sometimes a matter of survival. We choose not to know because in our industrialized world it's inconvenient; we choose not to know because we are afraid or exhausted or because we are suffering from such a severe lack of imagination that we can't picture a way out, so we don't want to know that we need one.

That lack of imagination, and our fear of the questions that come with it, can kill us.

Especially when we're intensives.

Because we're intensives, mental health issues are very likely to be mission-critical. The dead end that we think we see can feel completely real, and we're used to being right. Being used to being right means that it might not even occur to us that we're wrong. And we might, especially at first, reject out of hand anyone who tells us differently.

Our tendency to extremes works against us here.

Fie on that.

One of the most useful habits of thought I've ever developed is this: When you can only see two options, you're not seeing everything. You're missing something.

That goes double when the two options are: "Be miserable or die."

Nope nope nope.

Gotta be another way.

It's like you're an explorer. Maybe you're looking for the Holy Grail or something. You and your team are deep in the jungle or lost in the desert. You stumble across a cave that turns out to be a tunnel full of booby traps. You cleverly make it past the poisoned arrows and the snake pit and the giant, bone-crushing boulder. The tunnel changes; the air gets clearer. The floor slants upward. All of a sudden, you hear a thunderous roar, and there's a rockslide behind you. The way out is blocked. You're way underground. Radios are useless. And as you round a corner, there's a solid stone wall in front of you.

Now what?

Either you give up or you assume there's a way out.

If you assume there's a way out, either you start flinging yourself desperately at the stone wall, prying at the tons of rubble behind you, or...

Or...

You slowly, gently, delicately start palpating the wall in front of you. Your fingers trace every seam with the sensitivity of a surgeon's touch. You're looking for that thing that's ever so slightly different from the way it should be. You don't even know what you're looking for, but it's something.

And when you find the loose stone in the wall, it pivots silently and the whole wall swings open.

Victory.

But you have to be willing to *feel*, even if you don't know what good it will do.

You have to be able to wait for the panic to ebb so you can think. You have to be able to assume that there's another answer: You just haven't found it yet.

When there are only two options, your imagination is misfiring.

As intensives, we have an extra challenge: We are so used to dismissing our "crazy ideas" that we might have already seen the other options and discarded them as impossible or unrealistic or hopeless. Folks, we are intensives. We *specialize* in unrealistic. We are accustomed to having to make the reality that accommodates our imaginations. It's only when we have been trying to think like expansives for too long that we get completely stuck. We end up feeling like our job is to fit in, and that shrinks our willingness to push the edges of what people think is possible—and that is what keeps our best gifts locked, as it were, in the cupboard under the stairs.

I bought and framed a greeting card years ago that said, "Those who say it cannot be done should not interrupt the person doing it." The credit is "Chinese proverb" and, who knows, maybe it is. But whoever said it first, it is the intensive's motto.

We don't put much stock in the limitations imposed by history. We believe in an expanding future. We create more space as we go. It's who we are.

But that future vision is often on a toggle switch. If you become tired and irritated or if you are told eight times a week or an hour that the future isn't like that and you're not like that, you might get stubborn or—unfortunately more likely—you might get beaten down and stop believing in your own vision.

4 – 4

COMMUNITY

We need each other.

Just like introverts need to know other introverts, geeks need other geeks, and fashionistas need other people to understand the importance of just the right lip gloss and shoes, intensives need each other.

Because in each other's company, we thrive. We spend a lot of time getting really excited and saying things like, "RIGHT?" And "I KNOW!" And "ME TOO!" We dream dreams that make other people's heads explode. We are dynamite together. And we can spot the bullshit a mile away, and we can call it out and keep going.

We do not believe in limits while a project is in development.

They are not useful at that stage.

In fact, we only begrudgingly give into them at *all*.

We do our most brilliant work in each other's company, alternating with deep periods of immersion in our own projects. Over time we learn not to talk with most expansives until we're ready to show our work to the world. Expansives are often really uncomfortable with the size and scope of what we can see. But they call it "being realistic." We learn, over time, that this is toxic to us. Instead, if you want to think big, THINK BIG.

Stay away from people who will pare down your dreams.

In the old tellings of *Cinderella*, the two stepdaughters, trying to fit their feet into the glass slipper, cut off a toe and a heel, respectively. They get found out and brought back, but the toe is gone; the heel is gone. You cannot fit yourself into the wrong thing. They should never have listened to their mother, who felt that their only chance for success was to pretend to be someone they weren't. It's an appalling side narrative. Imagine living like that, constantly told that you had to be different. I imagine the stepsisters were wired for gardening and dressmaking or something like that, but the stepmother wanted them to be nobles and made mistake after mistake in trying to force them to be something they weren't. Trying to be something you're not, day in and day out for sixteen or eighteen years, can make you ugly inside and out.

Go barefoot in the dirt. To hell with the glass slipper and the prince, unless your foot actually fits. If your foot fits, then that's who you are, regardless of your rags.

It is *vitally important* that you not hide parts of yourself, even if no one around you understands them. You must find places and people to celebrate with. Don't stop looking until you find them. You might find groups or chats on social media, blogs, events, gatherings, sports or other activities, anything that attracts intensives. Go there.

So what's the good news?

The good news is that you have choices, you have tools, and you don't live in the era when you'd be considered possessed by the devil (or you can at least get a second opinion).

The better news is, if you're reading this, you know you have those things.

The *best* news is, once you get one toehold, it builds on itself.

So do what you need to do to get your toehold.

- Call a hotline.

- Write in your journal.

- Write a novel.

- Make art.

- Go hiking.

- Get a second job.

But whatever it is, be yourself in it. Don't squish yourself, don't fry yourself. Be yourself, and work toward more places where you can be yourself more often.

Spend more time around people who get you. If you're an intensive, gather intensives into your circle and *be deliberate about it.* I guarantee you are not alone, and some other intensive is going to be *elated* to discover that you exist.

Remember: You don't have to be healed or healthy or perfectly fixed or even imperfectly fixed to help someone. You have no idea when you're helping someone.

But you've got to *be here* to help someone.

That's it.

Just be.

4 – 5
GO BIG OR GO HOME...
OR NOT

M y father ran marathons for most of my life. Every morning he would rise in the dark, strap on his sneakers, and slip out the door, key tied to his shoelace. He had a four-mile route and a seven-mile route for everyday runs, and then a thirteen-mile route that he would build on for pre-race work.

For a couple of years I aspired to join him, but he couldn't bend his training schedule to match the needs of an eight-year-old and I couldn't quite get myself to run enough alone. We did one race together, a 5K, and then I stopped.

For years now, a 5K has felt completely out of reach. I have been out of shape, injured, and so on—and that was that. I also have some problems with body-temperature maintenance, which become a real problem when I exercise.

Unless, I discovered two summers ago, I want to swim.

I live near a shallow beach that is perfect for swimming. Every summer we're inundated with tourists, who are excellent for the local economy and generally not terrible for anything else.

I love getting in the water, but a few summers ago I discovered that I actually *love to swim*. After a summer of that discovery, I set off willy-nilly to swim to the next town.

I think it's about a mile, maybe a mile and a half. I set my rules: no putting my feet down, but I could tread or float as much as I wanted. I could choose whether to swim back. No rush, no time limit.

I did it. With no formal prep, I *just did it*.

There are physiological reasons why I can swim an ocean mile and not run a land mile, but for now I'll just say that a smaller goal wasn't possible to give me a sense of accomplishment. Far more important was the moment when I figured out how to do rotary breathing (in the middle of the swim), but what felt like something was the swimming itself.

When I was a kid I thought maybe someday I'd do an Ironman triathlon. Not just any triathlon, an Ironman. Because that's how the best of the best do it.

I wasn't willing to consider just swimming a little bit—or giving myself credit for what I *did* do.

Very occasionally this mindset makes sense, like when I say I *have to* write before ten in the morning or it won't happen. That's kind of a systemic absolute for me, one I've discovered over many years of trying to be productive at other times of day. That's recognizing my own patterns of genius and limitation.

But that's the exception. Usually things are not nearly as absolute as we make them out to be.

But we're intensives, so we do this to ourselves. We set goals that are *huge* and then either do that or do nothing at all. It's not a great routine. As the saying goes: "How do you eat an elephant? One bite at a time." Far smarter would be to adopt just a little bit of the expansive method and nibble reasonable bits until we've eaten the whole elephant. That's how I wrote the second half of this book.

But that's usually not us. We want to eat the elephant whole.

This can be unrealistic, this can be disastrous, or this can be sheer genius.

Our best move is to figure out when it is sheer genius and when it is not—ahead of time. Failing that, our job is to admit the disasters and abort those missions as soon as possible.

When something is *supposed* to take a while, that can be hard to discern.

Finding the places where productive stress give way to destructive stress and anxiety is absolutely key to surviving and eventually thriving. If you grew up with stress as a normative undertone, it can take a while to even notice there's a problem. But if you don't notice stress on your own, your system (your body, or your family and friends and colleagues) will eventually bring it to your attention, and it might not be pleasant.

You can get permanently anxious. You can get get adrenal fatigue. You can be tired all the time even though you're eating right, exercising, and getting enough sleep. You can get cranky. You can start eating all the wrong foods for your body. You can get a chronic cough or cold. You can get tight muscles that make no ergonomic sense. The list goes on and on.

If you're going spelunking for clues, try rolling back to things that you thought were normal when you were a kid that you later figured out were considered a bit odd. They might be intensiveness markers, or they might be indications that something was wrong and you were managing it the best way you could.

When I was a kid, I loved to get up early. Not all intensives do this—some are night owls, we even have the occasional midday beacon—but I *loved* early. If I got up early enough, the house was still quiet—still safe. Being safe came from everyone else sleeping. If the window was open I probably heard birds, but what I remember is the quiet, my breath already held behind my teeth, stepping silently into the day. I learned to open my door so it didn't creak, tiptoe quiet-quiet-quiet into the bathroom, not pee yet, not yet not yet—although anxiety would get me eventually. (I found out a few years ago that morning diarrhea isn't normal; who knew?)

Still.

My father got up early, too, to run in the dusky streets before the day had quite begun. Later he would put on his slacks, blazer, and tie, in an odd mimicry of the kind and gentle Mr. Rogers. He was always on a strict schedule for work; everyone had to work like clockwork so he could be out the door on time. Often his tea was too hot but he was committed, pouring it in long streams from cup to cup over the sink until he could gulp it down.

It never occurred to me that this was odd.

Early mornings meant safety: I could do my own routine and get a little ahead of schedule and no one minded. I could be safe in the knowledge that I would be on time for the unpredictable and chaotic bus.

But here's the thing: I wanted to be *earliest*. I wanted to be earlier than anyone else. If my father was up at si,x I wanted five-thirty. Sure, part of that was being the only person awake. But part of it was doing it more, doing it better, being the best early-getter-up-per. There was no *reason* for me to need or want to be that early. I just did. In school, I wanted the hardest teachers. I took French in part because people said it was harder than Spanish….but also because *people who wanted easy were taking Spanish.* And I knew *they* were not my people.

Now, even now, I struggle with this. I *do* want ease. I've gotten over this weird machismo. But I also want challenge. There's no virtue in struggle just for struggle's sake. If struggle comes, then yes, it will help the wings of the butterfly fill with blood. But you're not a damn butterfly, and sometimes you just want things to be easeful. Lovely and easeful.

Creating conflict is often a way for us to replicate the conditions we are most familiar with. The ease of knowing-what-to-do trumps the ease of knowing-it's-okay.

Frankly, that's a little fucked up.

Over time, constant stress rewires our brains and changes our brain chemistry until we are literally addicted to the stress chemicals. We have more receptors for them and fewer receptors for the chemistry of happiness, so we will actually create stress to make those receptors happy.

It takes a *lot* of deconditioning and reconditioning to change that. But slowly, slowly, we come back from the brink, until one morning we wake up and we're not already anxious, our hearts are beating at a normal rate, and weu're okay with doing things in the way that makes the most sense, which might actually be easy.

It doesn't have to be hard. It doesn't have to be nearly as hard as we make it for ourselves. In the chapter about daily life I talked about New England and our particular habit of believing that everything is better when it's hard. It's not.

Here's the problem: we can do it. We can take the hardest trail to the top and make it work. We kind of like the challenge. But every time we do that, it takes energy. As intensives, we are best off when we choose where to use our energy and where to let it be okay that we didn't toil all day over a hot stove.

When you take the easy way, you leave yourself more resources to do the hard stuff when it really matters. I used to think I didn't need to work smarter-not-harder; I could work hard all the time.

Sure. I can.

Sometimes it's okay to be easy. And it's okay for it to be easy.

If you're an intensive, the odds are that you're incredibly gifted at something—that along the way to wherever you are, you got obsessive enough and in love enough and serious enough about at least one thing that you got good at it, but part of your love affair, where it started, is that it was a gift anyway. You might not think of it as a gift—you probably think of it as "can't everyone do that?" The answer is no, not everyone can do that. Certainly not the everyone that we all know and love. You're special. And claiming that you're not is kind of mean. Because if you're not special, then no one is and it's just hard work that separates you from Baryshnikov, and I don't think you actually believe *that* unless your gift is dance.

Whatever you do that's as easy as breath, that's your gift—and in a classic fish-in-the-water-don't-know-they're-wet move, this is a place where your usually impeccable self-awareness fails you. Only you're not used to having it fail, so you don't believe it's failing. So you think everyone can do that.

Nope.

Just for the record.

So what can you (and we) do once we've figured all this out?

For one thing, we can stop assuming that people around us are willfully failing to keep up. That person who didn't do the thing that would just have taken a minute? It probably would have taken them an hour. Stop using your own capacity as a litmus test. It's not fair.

For another thing, when we can't keep up with people (in my case, literally, sometimes), we can cut ourselves slack. Not everyone can do everything, so if something is hard, it's hard. Not your gift, that's all.

We can give ourselves permission to do some things badly, just for the joy of it. You're probably used to being pretty damn good at everything you do. But if you let yourself do things that are hard for you at first, there's a special kind of satisfaction in mastering something that doesn't come easily. You're probably not used to going after that, because there's so much of the other, fast satisfaction available. I'm not saying don't use your gifts. Please use them! The world needs you to use them. You need to use them. But allow room for doing-it-badly-but-doing-it-anyway activities. As I've mentioned before, I let myself try painting when I was in my late twenties. It's delightful, and I do it for fun. I don't sell my work. I don't know a thing about light or color theory that I didn't pick up in eighth-grade art class. I don't care. That's not the point. When I get too obsessive about getting it "right" I stop making art. I don't *want* to stop making art. Paint is *fun*. *That's* the point. There's a whole world that opens up when you stop having to be good at things, because you learn that frustration and dead ends aren't the end of the world. Sometimes just showing up at the studio or the page day after day is all it takes. And sometimes you can find a different way to be taught.

Reaching for things is good. Being unsure of yourself is good. Going outside your usual suspects is good.

That doesn't mean you should stop looking for the best way to do it. When I got the bit in my teeth about learning calculus, it took me three tries to pass the class. For me, that was ridiculous. It *never* takes me that many tries to learn something. But math and I do not have a good history. I was determined, however, not to fail. I failed twice on my way there, but I did eventually pass. However, the way I passed had everything to do with me thinking about *why* it was so hard. When I figured it out finally, it was because I was so annoyed that it was taking me so long to succeed. I went to my professor, explained what I had figured out about my own learning style, and made specific requests about how he could approach teaching me. Because I was at an excellent college with an emphasis on good teaching, he listened, and we worked together on it. I like to think it continued to inform his teaching long after I graduated.

So don't stop being curious about ways it could be different, but don't assume it *has* to be different. Whatever you want to do can be done for the pure joy of it, and not in the hardest or most virtuosic way possible. I want to take up horseback riding. I have no interest in competition. I want to ride trails and have a horse-friend. So I'll keep looking until I find a barn that will help me do it that way.

It's also important to balance your intuition, which is super-strong, with *just letting someone else be right.* Letting other people be right isn't a strong suit of intensives. We tend to be right a lot, and we tend to be sure we're right even more often than that. But by practicing things that we're not gifted at, we give ourselves the chance to relax into someone else's leadership and expertise. For an hour or a day or a weekend, someone else is in charge. We don't have to leap in to make things run better. We don't have to have or find answers. On the other hand, sometimes we're right even when we don't know much.

At one point I was considering horseback riding at a barn where something just felt…*off.* As it turned out, *several* things were off. It was good for me to follow my instinct and remove myself from the situation. I didn't have to be an expert in horsemanship to feel the dissonance. The key is balance. It took me a few weeks to decide, because I'm not an expert. But over time you learn the difference between "this feels wrong" and "good God I'm so frustrated with this that I could chew nails."

4 – 6
Problems

O bsession with problems is probably not a problem.

One day I was up early. The heat had been malfunctioning for a few days, and I had just figured out what's wrong. Or at least I had started to figure it out—which meant that I hadn't slept since 4:45. That's not great, but for that day at least, it wasn't terrible. And I was trying something to fix the problem, having finally fixed another problem with my phone so I could read about loop hot water baseboard heat on Google.

We tend to obsess about problems, we intensives. As children, when we asked questions, we were frequently hushed or told to look up the answer. We learned over time that it would bug us *forever*, so we now go straight to Google, no passing Go or collecting $200.

The random research rabbit holes are tricky, but the justifiable ones are far trickier. "I'm doing research to solve the problem," we tell ourselves. "It's important." "It's not like I'm wasting *time*."

Riiiiight. We want to be experts on everything. Sometimes we *are* wasting time because we don't like to be at a disadvantage when we call the real experts. Like the heat guy.

But sometimes we develop a theory that makes some amount of sense.

And sometimes even if it doesn't make sense, it makes more sense than thumb-twiddling, and you never know we might be right and at least we're doing *something* and if this doesn't work maybe if we tweak that thing…

So okay, maybe eventually it makes no sense. Just call an expert. But for a while anyway it works out okay.

For a while, we're good. *For a while.*

We like to know, because we like to be in control. But it's really much easier when we surrender. When we don't, we find ourselves facing down the intensified versions of anxiety and stress: anger, depression, and the thing that feels like a tool but isn't, addiction.

4 – 7

INTENSIVES AND ANGER

Perhaps this would be better entitled "Intensives and Fury."

We can get *so* angry.

One time I was describing my anger to a psychiatrist and he insisted on putting me on antipsychotics for a few days.

I didn't need antipsychotics. For one thing, they didn't help. For another thing, I wasn't even slightly psychotic. (Other therapists confirmed this almost immediately). I was just *mad*. Our culture doesn't have a lot of room for women to get mad. Certainly not furious. But when we *are* that mad, it's important for us to be able to express it.

I have a friend who has been through a terrible series of experiences, compounded by a dreadful miscarriage of justice. Recently I spoke with them on the phone.

They are *furious*. Their fury scares even them. But when you have been raised and acculturated as a woman, there is no acceptable expression of that fury.

Our anger can be so big it scares even us. We can have fantasies and rages that would horrify people out of context. Like everything else we feel, it can temporarily drown out our surroundings and become the only thing we're aware of.

(By the way, if energy work is your thing, you know that this kind of anger can feel like a terrible focusing of energy, ready to lash out. I learned as a child that touching people when I was angry felt like a universally bad idea.)

There are a few problems with feeling scared about your anger— most notably that you're likely to suppress it, which can lead to all kinds of emotional and physical fallout. If you have chronic muscle tension without a clear physical cause, for example, it's likely that you're holding your anger in those muscles.

No wonder you don't want to relax, because if that anger gets out, who knows who could be hurt?

But here's the thing: *Anger is simply focused power*, in the same way that money is power. We have lots of stories about what money is and what anger is, but all of it boils down to a discomfort with power. People who are comfortable with their own power are typically comfortable with anger or money, sometimes both.

If you imagine anger as power that has been rounded up and aimed at injustice (perceived or real), then you can start to see its utility. I won't even begin to claim that it's harmless, because it most certainly is not. Power isn't power if it can't create change, and the risk of agency is that you'll create change that is somehow harmful. That's part of the deal. But you don't need to be scared of that—just aware and responsible. Having anger is like driving a car; having fierce anger is like driving a car on the freeway. You have to be more aware to stay safe, that's all.

And you *can* be safe.

Often (especially if we grew up with one or more intensive parents) we have experienced anger being unsafe, which we might extrapolate to *all* anger being unsafe. Which couldn't be farther from the truth.

Part of the role of anger is to keep us safe. And in a matrix with other senses and sensibilities, we can arrange things so that we get to stay safe while also keeping other people safe *and* getting our needs met.

Because that's what safety is: getting our minimum needs met. Comfort is getting a little more than the minimum. Luxury and abundance mean getting a *lot* more than the minimum. Anger kicks in when we look like we're getting near the bottom of the barrel.

Now, to some extent that's true for everyone, not just intensives.

But for us, the anger can be big. *Really* big. (If it's mixed with an old experience of trauma, that's another story. There are lots of things that can overlap with intensiveness that have their own stories and conditions. Trauma is one of them.)

When the anger is big, it's because our internal power is getting focused and revved up. We're getting ready to go into battle. The ancient Celts used to sprint downhill into a battle, swords raised, screaming at the tops of their lungs. They won a lot of battles on the strength of that charge. Nothing like a panicked enemy for confusion and chaos.

But in modern contexts, that whole battle can happen inside you, with equally devastating results. When you try to contain your rage instead of finding a good way to express it, you panic. The rage isn't meant to be contained. It's too big for your insides. And you can trigger yourself, setting off intense emotional cascades that harken back to old, unhealed wounds or simply to primal survival instincts that limit your capacity to respond well.

But you can't escape.

Sometimes that kind of internalized anger can lead to depression.

Sometimes it just leads to confusion.

Or stress.

Or self-destructive behaviors.

It's kind of like an autoimmune disorder, only instead of immunity as we usually understand it, it's mental immunity to the cruelty and stupidity of the world. Eventually, activated but with no outlet, it attacks its host body. (That would be you.)

So what can we do with this *giant supersized rage* that we get when something isn't right?

Often, we Do Something. We retool the system, write a letter, start a new institution. We fix it the best way we can. That kind of planning helps to diffuse the anger, because we're working on a way to *cure* the thing we see as a disease. This is how so many of us end up as inventors, entrepreneurs, and activists.

But what if, for whatever reason, you can't? What then?

1. **Get yourself witnessed.** Rage in solitude is way less satisfying than rage with an audience. Find a close friend you really, really trust who is not triggered by anger, and ask them to listen to you vent as long as you need to. (Set a timer: two hours is about the longest most people can go.) Say all the horrible, cruel, scary, furious things you need to say. Get them heard. Get them out there.

2. **Move your body.** The body chemistry that comes up with big rage is meant for battling lions and Escaping

leopards on the savanna. It doesn't dissipate when you sit still, and it makes all your internal systems get twisty. Do something that takes a lot of large muscle work: stack wood, run (sprint), rock climb, until you're exhausted. Then be prepared to really rest.

3. If you can't find someone to witness you, **write a letter** that you might never send. Say everything you want to say.

4. **Scream.** If you have a place where you can go where no one will get scared, go ahead and shout or scream your way through it.

5. **Do some art you're bad at.** I have no training in painting or drawing, so that's my go-to when I need unrestricted expression. Dance is good, music is good—anything you can give yourself complete freedom on. Bonus points if it involves large muscle groups (see item 2).

And then let it be okay to let it go.

When I'm angry or sad I often feel like, if I allow myself to release it, I'm going to forget the importance of whatever caused the problem—worrying, for example, that I will forget someone who died if I don't stay in grief.

Nothing could be less true.

The anger is what allows us to move forward. We can't make the best of the tragedy or loss unless we move through the anger spike so we can think again. We can stay aware and energized and focused without losing all of our higher-order thinking—which is what happens when we get so angry. All the parts of the brain not involved in basic-level functioning just shut down. Moving through the spike allows us access to creative thinking, our sense of humor, and complex idea formation. Those are the things that allow us to form long-term solutions to the problem at hand.

In an NPR interview, Shonda Rimes said, "Power isn't power if you don't know you have it." But when you know you have it, you have to be comfortable holding it and willing to wield it, or it just eats you up from the inside out. Anger is just a form of power. And, as Ani DiFranco sang, "Every tool is a weapon if you hold it right."

The question is, do you need a sword? Or do you need a plow?

Sometimes the anger stays directed outward. Sometimes it goes inward. There are lots of reasons for that. It's easier. It feels safer. It feels like if there's something wrong with you, then you control the problem and you can fix it (which you do, but not in the way you think you do when you're depressed).

Naturally, when we get depressed, we do that intensely, too. In fact, mental illness of all kinds seems to be more severe for us. We just go all-in. Unfortunately, with fatal diseases, all-in can be all-dead. If you have depression, I cannot say this loudly enough: *Get help*. Get a therapist—start there. Explore all the options. You never know where relief will come from. Your brain is powerful, and that power can save your life. Or it can kill you.

I will also say this: Often part or all of our depression comes from trying to make ourselves too small. Squishing yourself into a "normal" (expansive) mold when you're an intensive is potentially fatal, and I'm not exaggerating. If you are in an environment where you're forever being told that you're too much, too big, too loud, too wild, too whatever, your brain chemistry is getting changed, your brain structure is getting changed, you're getting beaten down and the result can be devastating. Don't blow it off. don't tell yourself to get used to it or get over it. *Get out*.

GET THE FUCK OUT.

You think you can do it. You think you can handle it. You think it will be okay. *You are wrong.* You are killing yourself, starting by causing diseased structures in your brain that lead to problematic thinking and feeling patterns. Those patterns, over time, will destroy you.

I AM NOT KIDDING.

And yes, I'm shouting. Because I've been through it, and I've watched loved ones go through it. It is horrifying. From the outside, it looks like someone torturing themselves to death to make someone else happy. Only, if they love you, it *doesn't* make them happy, because they know on some level how miserable you are.

From the inside, you think you're doing the best thing, using your intensity to moderate your intensity. It'll be okay, you think. I'll just stab myself a little. I'll just pull the trigger a little.

Take the gun away from your head.

Sheath the dagger and the sword.

Put down the weapons and walk away.

You do not deserve to die.

Much less by your own hand.

You need to be yourself in order to be mentally healthy. You need to be as big, as bold, as wild, as loving, as connected, as real as you are wired to be. You need room to move. You need a place for all the vast brilliance of you.

Fall deeply in love with your intensity. It's the only way. If you can't love it, you can't be you.

This is a time when the surrender you need is not to depression, not to what's directly in front of you, but what's to the left, just out of range of your vision. The surrender you need is to the delight of who you are. If you can't see it, get help. Get friends or lovers or therapists or coaches to help you hold that image in your mind's eye until you can see it clearly, because if you can turn your focus that way, you'll turn the whole ship.

4 – 8

INTENSIVES AND ADDICTION

When you're intense, you tend to do things all the way, all the time—more than most people think you could or should. More than most people can imagine. And when you find something you *really* like, you do it even more than that. It scares off lovers, it leads to brilliant insights at work, it makes us over- or underachievers in school…and it makes us *way* more likely to be addicts.

We find something we like and we *do* it.

We are already used to ignoring the people in our lives who tell us that we shouldn't be doing something that much, so we miss the social cues. We trust ourselves to handle more than the average person, so we ignore the warnings. And then, suddenly, there we are.

The good news is, there we are. We can notice and we can change. The bad news is, something has to happen *to us* to get us to change. That thing could be an accident, a bad relationship moment, a bad night. But we tend to require personal experience with the badness. Seeing it happen to someone we know is rarely sufficient.

We tend to think of ourselves as unique. It helps us do the crazy things no one thinks we can do, but it also keeps us from recognizing where we are actually quite similar to others and where their vulnerabilities reflect ours.

There's healthy obsession and then there's the rest of it.

Seeing ourselves when we're not perfect can be painful until we've really mastered surrender—and sometimes even then.

We don't like seeing our vulnerabilities. We don't like acknowledging our vulnerabilities. We like to pretend that we are superheroes, because sometimes, with our intensity at full volume, we can fake it for a minute.

But we aren't superheroes, and there is little better suited to demonstrating that than our vulnerability to addiction.

Because we feel things so intensely, we are likely to seek ways of dulling that experience when it becomes too much. Even with our elevated thresholds, we all have our limits, especially for the unpleasant side of things.

Some of us manage to find relatively healthy distractions or obsessions, but not all of us do. Those of us who don't often turn to smoking, alcohol, pot—anything to slow us down and take the edge off.

And, as in the rest of our lives, if a little is good, a lot is better, right?

Open door, enter addiction stage right.

Addictions make things easier. We can rationalize the hell out of anything, so a substance that makes us more relaxed, nicer to the people around us, and helps us sleep or helps our brains spin down after they get revved up? Sounds like it's more helpful than harmful, right?

But if we're not dealing with the underlying causes, if we're not being honest with ourselves, if we're stuck in a life or a job or a career that we are so unsuited to that we really should be trying to escape...

We're going to try to escape our reality, and addictions are a slippery slope into what feels like comfort and ease.

We *like* comfort and ease.

We like things that feel like they help us.

We like to make our own decisions.

We like to feel independent.

We're rebellious by nature.

But we hate being out of integrity, and that will eventually get us. If we're unlucky, the addiction will kill us before we can get to it. If we're lucky, we'll catch it.

We will find people who love us the way we are. Supportive community where you can be real and be yourself and not act on your addictions is, in fact, the opposite of addiction.

In terms of intensive behavior patterns, recognized addictions like drugs and alcohol take their place right next to less recognized ones involving food and work and zoning out in front of the TV and constantly refreshing social-media websites. Sometimes these things have a purpose for a little while, but rarely does that purpose extend to an obsession that interferes with the rest of our lives.

So we hit that point where we can numb ourselves out or we can choose to live.

There is good news, though: We can be as fierce at getting or staying off of something as we are about getting onto it. Once we know we are changing, we tend to set course as fiercely as ever. We are the people who go cold turkey, or who have never been drunk in the first place. We tend not to seek middle ground when we are truly ready for a change. As the AA *Big Book* reads, when "half-measures avail us nothing," we can avail ourselves of the whole thing and go all-in on getting better.

Things can go badly.

Things can go *really* badly.

But we have the skills and the stubbornness to match it. It's all in our heads, and when we can separate the dismay and despair from the intensiveness, we can hitch that power to a different wagon and tow ourselves out of the mud.

We need to do it. It's not an indulgence. It's not a weakness.

We need to be happy, we intensives.

Richard Branson has been known to say, "I am not happy because I'm successful, I am successful because I am happy."

We feel things deeply all the time: sadness, happiness, frustration, shame, pride, guilt, joy, delight, pleasure. And these things affect our work.

We are the temperamental artists, the eccentric inventors, the crazy-but-brilliant or the crazy-but-crazy. There is almost always genius in us somewhere. Whether we have turned it to recognizably good use or not is something else entirely.

But when we are unhappy, we are terrible. We can be destructive; we can be moody; it takes a fair bit of inner training to get us to the point where we can merely create violent works of art instead of being violent toward our creations. If we are compassionate, and most of us are, we misguidedly take ourselves out of the company of those we love when we are unhappy. Mix that with depression and it can spell some major isolation.

But mostly we don't know what else to *do* with ourselves.

Our culture doesn't really teach us this, but there's a lot to learn that can help. We're not used to learning like that. We're used to intuiting half and picking up the rest on the fly, and being good at it, whatever it is. So we tend to resist things that require intense study unless we have become obsessed with them. But this is one of those places where that doesn't serve us. It can be really useful to go to a workshop (or a therapist, or both) and actually learn what we need to know so we can manage our own moods without being destructive or isolated.

Usually it's fine to see ourselves and our feelings as a single unit. That's how we fly so fast—because we don't perceive a separation between the pilot and the craft. But when the autopilot program crashes at 30,000 feet, you need a plan B. Plan B is to have a person-pilot, a written flight plan, training for the instrument panel.

When the autopilot crashes, you hit manual override and take a deep breath. Then you take over the controls and stabilize the craft while you run down the checklist and figure out what went wrong.

That training—the training to write a flight plan, the training to understand the instrument panel and, ultimately, to fly the damn plane—is available. And if you want to be responsible for anyone except yourself, it can save your ass. Learning this means:

- Learn to notice what you're feeling. You can learn this from a therapist or at a personal growth workshop

- Learn what the next possibilities are; learn to look for all the options. Most of us feel and act immediately out of that feeling, or we stuff the feeling down and intellectualize our way out of the situation. Those are two choices, but there are more. You can feel the feeling, name it, and then pause and choose. That's a very powerful move, not least because most people don't do that. It also means you're not acting under the ninety-second wash of adrenaline and cortisol that keeps you from using your higher-order thinking.

- Learn to CHOOSE what you do with that feeling. Some coaches, therapists, and workshops can teach this as well.

- Learn to stay nimble. Especially under stress, humans tend to get rigid about their choices. Don't fall victim to that. It's brain chemistry and habit, but don't let it be in control. Stay nimble, take in new information, keep watching, keep learning, iterate.

- Consider all the factors in your situation. This is a hard one, because that ninety seconds of panic chemistry literally and figuratively narrows your vision. You have to ride it out until your vision widens again and consider things like what goals you might have in common with your loved ones. When it comes to managing depression and/or bad moods, communicating clearly with those around you is helpful; asking for support is, too. Discomfort can make us stiff and demanding. It helps a lot if we can learn to access another option—the soft vulnerability that lets us not lash out at the people who love us. The autopilot wants to crash every plane at once. We need to make a different choice.

- Celebrate the successes. Really celebrate. It's important. I know you're very busy—we all are, it's part of what makes us intensives and it's part of what makes us successful—but when something works, schedule a day to do the success right. Review the story of your success over and over. Talk to people about it. Look at it closely: What led up to the success? When did you make right moves at critical moments? We do this all the time with failures. We are not wired to do it for successes. (Getting a drink of water without getting chased by a lion, no big deal. Getting chased by a lion? Better remember the details so it never happens again.) We need to override that wiring, because otherwise our successes fade into the background.

This is probably the single most important skillset I teach my clients: not to let the bad days, bad moods, ot depression into the pilot's seat, but to see the situation, breathe through the initial adrenaline, and make a conscious choice about the next step. It takes practice. They slip, they misstep, we try again. The better you get, the better it gets.

The cost of losing the pilot's seat can be a half-day or a half-week of craziness, and that's if we don't manage to crash the plane for real.

How do we know when we need to switch from autopilot to manual?

Knowing yourself, your triggers and your red flags, is really helpful. Make a chart: What happens when you're slipping into a funk? What happens that tends to send you into a funk?

If calling your mother is a triggering event, set conditions for it and bookend it with other activities. Don't call when you're tired, disoriented, or already feeling grumpy. Set a time limit for the conversation. Make an appointment with someone else right afterward so (a) you have an excuse to end the conversation and (b) you will have something to cheer you up and change your brain state.

But funk-slippage can happen over a long period of time, too. Classic symptoms of depression can also be symptoms of not-quite-depression-but-damn-this-sucks: losing interest in your hobbies, ignoring your loved ones, neglecting maintenance tasks, anything where you say "I don't care" a lot, snarking about everyone around you, drowning your sorrows. The marks of unhealthy use include *knowing you shouldn't* and doing it anyway.

If you notice these kinds of things in yourself, it's time to take over the controls. The autopilot is beginning to slip. For a while, don't let your feelings run the show. Do things you know will help. If you don't know what might help, a therapist or coach or both can probably help with that. You're smart. Under the funk is a perfectly capable pilot, and if you consult *that* pilot (not the one who wants to crash the plane) you will find that you are perfectly aware if what you are dealing with is depression or just a bad mood. Act accordingly.

Make no mistake: Depression is a potentially fatal disease. Treat it like you would cancer. Bad moods are not fatal, but they still merit your attention, because (and this is important) *any* mood disruption is magnified by your intensity and will directly affect your productivity. You may be able to get by at work on half-performance because you're still better than three-quarters of the people there. But you *know* you're not meeting your own standard, and it eats at you. It adds to the funk. Compound funk is way more draining than compound interest. Don't let it take your best ideas and inspirations away from you. Your risk tolerance is one of the most powerful things about you. Make sure it can shine and not become part of the problem.

This is not to say you should learn to control your emotions. Emotions are vital to proper functioning. Rather, you should learn to know that your emotions are present, learn to see them, and learn to decide if they should be running the show. When you're doing well, it's a major asset. But when you feel like shit, there are other options. Use them.

A note on intersecting diagnoses:

There are a few things that people frequently ask about as they relate to intensiveness: bipolar disorder, ADHD, obsessive-compulsive disorder, and autism spectrum disorder.

I am not a doctor.

I can only say that I have met people who have been diagnosed with these things and are intensive, and I have met people who have not been diagnosed with these things and do not appear to have these things, and are intensive.

I do not think I have any of them, and I am intensive.

If you think you or your child may have a condition like those listed above, please, please, please see a professional. This book is in no way a diagnostic tool or guide.

4 – 9
CASE STUDY

When my friend Xavier asked me to work with him, he had been searching for years.

He knew he wasn't who he wanted to be.

He knew something was wrong, but for the life of him he couldn't find the solution, and neither could anyone else. He was vaguely but dangerously discontent, sliding between apathy and depression in an alarming fashion.

And he was carrying an ideal that felt impossibly far away: He wanted to be the kind of guy who gets the girls, has a ton of money, and is still a great person with good values.

Oh, and he wanted to be in a completely different body.

Initially we tried regular spoken coaching. We tried some energy work. We tried bodywork. We tried a lot of things, and kept running into absolutely intractable barriers.

Then we tried the thing that had been my ideal for years, but that I'd never been able to try: mixing them all together. Every skill, every talent, every training I had came into play. We used them all, sometimes several in a single session. It was deep, it was profound, it was rich. Most important, it was effective.

And it was over-the-top intense.

Xavier is an intensive with a few fringe expansive qualities, closer to the center than I am, but his deep desire to do this work made him more intensity-tolerant. The fact that we had been friends for several years made him more tolerant. Then the work actually started to change things for him. That was the biggest convincer of all.

So we went out on the skinny branches. We decided to do the work and run it as a beta test, an experiment, following it as far as it would go. As it turned out, it went as far as I had imagined, which was about three times farther than he had imagined.

His relationship to his sexuality changed.

His ability to move forward on almost everything that mattered to him changed.

Even his attitude about healthy eating, one of his most intractable issues, changed.

His relationship with his family matured and evolved.

As a result, his social life bloomed, his interpersonal skills bloomed, and his next career move emerged from the mists that had been hiding it.

So why did the work *work*?

Because his intensiveness was finally getting to come out and play. He had gotten into the habit of suppressing his intensity, to the point where he either didn't know it was there or carried an immense amount of shame and guilt about it. It meant that none of his gifts were getting full expression; often the ones that were at all visible were getting used for the wrong reasons, from obligation instead of from joy.

When I went in looking for the roots of shame, I found them in the closet, where his intensiveness had been left to rot.

Being closeted is very rarely the best choice. Making yourself into your own dirty little secret destroys you from the inside out.

If you are an intensive, you have a compelling need to let that shine. That's what this book is about: making intensity a fully integrated and beautiful gift that you use, share, and show off freely, instead of something that you pretend doesn't exist.

You're not like everyone else.

You're also not too much.

Intensity suits you. Show it off!

Xavier's transformation feels like some of the most important work I have ever done, because it revealed so much about the nature of intensives. We are pressure cookers. We have to do things to express ourselves or we explode.

But when we *can* express ourselves, we are the unbelievable dreamers your mother warned you about. We build things and do things that people think are impossible. We boldly go where no one has gone before. It's our thing. We don't hold things steady; we move them. Mostly forward. With a lot of force.

And when that force comes out sideways instead, it's not pretty.

We are more prone to mental health issues: depression, suicidality, anxiety, panic. We are smart enough to talk ourselves into more unlit and twisty dead ends and corners than other, people. We can convince ourselves we will never get out.

Or we can make a different choice.

Now I'm not (not *ever*) saying that depression is not a disease or that everyone should be able to think themselves out of it. I and many others have used some kind of help (for me it was homeopathy and therapy, but everyone is different) to recover.

Let me be very clear: *Whatever treatment it takes* to keep your brain healthy is the treatment you need.

Even with good treatment, there's a certain amount of internal work to be done, a certain amount of changing your brain that is required. Several of the chapters in this book offer tools that can help you shift the patterns that your brain is used to—patterns that can determine whether your intensiveness gets in your way or gets you going.

As an intensive you have an incredibly powerful brain. And you can decide that you aren't going to use it for convincing yourself of your unworthiness or for persuading yourself to let your depression drive. That is something you can *choose*—not to make it any easier for your brain to get all twisty.

Instead, you can bring your intensiveness to bear on your talent, your gifts for the world, letting your joy make your decisions. You can use it to strengthen your relationships, try new things, help people who need support or assistance, change the world.

You decide.

Making that decision, with the same bloody-minded stubbornness that you usually apply to doing something the world tells you cannot be done, will make a world of difference.

Try it and see.

PART FIVE

SAVING THE WORLD

5 – 1

SAVING THE WORLD

When I started to write this book, I had no notions about it saving the world. I thought I would talk a little bit about the experience I had, and the experiences of my friends and the people I'd contacted while writing the book. I thought I'd talk about something that kept showing up around the edges, around the margins, but never really got said. It's kind of the story of my life: that I say the thing that everyone is thinking (and no one is saying).

But the longer I worked with the material, the more I realized that my own biases were playing into it. This wasn't a problem that I was having just because I am different and have always been different, but that I was having this problem because I was part of a system that has inherent bias. *That* was interesting.

Dominant culture in the United States and Canada is powerfully biased in favor of expansives. By contrast, many historically marginalized cultures in the United States seem to have much more room for intensives. These include the Black, Irish, Italian, Jewish, Latinx, and (Asian) Indian populations and, in Canada, the French Canadians and Acadians. Any culture that gets accused of being too loud, too smelly, dancing too much, partying too late, and so on is probably an intensive-embracing culture. In order to gain traction in a place dominated by the expansive-oriented British-derived culture, most of the leaders we know of from other cultures muted their intensiveness. This dovetails interestingly with the work around intercultural competence and conflict styles (www. icsinventory.com).

When we intensives are into something, we're *into* it. We focus hard. We do that and nothing else. We feel deeply; we live with passion. We might be quiet or we might be exuberant, but we follow our ideas to their almost ridiculous conclusions.

In the dominant cultures of the United States, especially in New England, passion tends to be frowned upon, especially in public.

Subtlety is valued. Decorum, which is another way of saying "being quiet and still," is valued. There are rare contexts where you're allowed to express something different (like sports games), but most of the time, not.

The way to success in most places is to fit into the dominant culture.

If you're in a bank, act like a banker. If you're in New England, act like a New Englander. And when in Rome...

We intensives have been learning that we should fit in for a long time. If there are any saving graces, it's that the culture of the United States *also* encourages innovation and creativity, at least to some extent. We have room for eccentrics, and (ostensibly) for other cultures, and intensives often move toward eccentricity and difference.

We don't tend to work out well working for other people. We gravitate toward jobs and families and environments where we can be in charge—at least of ourselves, and ideally of our environment as well. As a result, middle-of-the-road, dominant, white US culture isn't generally where we do best.

However.

The United States is a place where vast numbers of cultures converge and, to some extent, mix. And while the culture with the most power over the last several hundred years has been white European and heavily British-influenced, it hasn't always been like that.

Before the occupation, Indigenous and Aboriginal peoples lived here, presumably with a diversity of values and modes of self-expression. This continent was richly populated with independent nations that interacted across their own cultural differences.

Then the Europeans came, eventually dominated by the British.

During British rule, people from other cultures were forcibly brought here and often enslaved. Those cultures tended to be more accepting of feelings and expressions of those feelings than the British were: of enthusiasm, of grief, of joy. There is a reason the British have such a reputation for a "stiff upper lip." It's valued in their culture. The British have one of the most expansive cultures in the world.

Because the British-dominated culture was expansive and the people they brought here under duress were brought as second-class, we developed over time a cultural association of intensiveness with "uncultured" or low class.

"Classy" has a sense of gracious and subtle. (Expansive.)

"Classless" has a sense of overbearing, sloppy, and blunt. (Intensive.)

So it goes.

Why is this relevant?

Because when intensives try to find a place in a society that thinks of intensity and intensiveness as inherently less-than and problematic, we have to do a lot of maneuvering to manage. As children, we are almost universally taught that we should "tone it down," "calm down," and certainly not bore Aunt Gertrude with all the details of Boston's transit system, even though that's our current obsession.

Perhaps Aunt Gertrude would have appreciated our enthusiasm, but she has also been taught that she can't talk about *her* favorite things willy-nilly, so it becomes a generational problem. She imposes the strictures she learned on the people she is raising, and the problem is passed down.

We are trained not to cry in public when we're moved; not to allow the energy to move us where it will; and, for heaven's sake, get up at six, eat at seven, leave for work at seven-thirty, be at your desk or station by eight, eat again at noon, work until five or six, and be home just in time for dinner.

We intensives usually *hate* being cogs in the wheel, although we can get a certain amount of satisfaction from being the Perfect Cog. Usually, though, we get bored. And a bored intensive gets creative, which can be dangerous.

Or it can be brilliant.

Dominant culture, though, tends to reward coggishness—with the exception of the dot-com boom and its attendant burst of entrepreneurial opportunities. Suddenly, there was a culturally acceptable way to innovate, stay up all night, and work like the devil is on your tail. Overnight, intensives found a place.

As it turns out, though, having one cultural group dominate in a confluence country with ideals of equality is maybe not such a great idea. People who were historically marginalized here almost all have the exuberance of culture in common, even the ones who are near neighbors to Britain: the Irish, the Italians, the Jews, the Indians, the several cultures from Africa. (The Japanese are a notable exception.)

The less enthusiastic, loud, and expressive a group can get, the more likely they are to rise to the top in the United States. Rising through the ranks requires pouring oneself into one mold after another to suit the people at the next level, until you get to the top.

Then?

You can tread water as an expansive, but to grow when there's no one over you, you're going to need to become at least a bit more intensive.

This is a fundamental crisis of leadership in this country. We raise people through the ranks for being expansive, but to lead, the more intensive they are, the better.

We need to stop teaching people to repress their intensive qualities. While a minority of us are intense enough to identify as intensives, most of us have some intensiveness, and for those who want to lead that needs to be cultivated, not suppressed.

We need to recognize that cultures that are more accepting of intensive qualities need to be encouraged, supported, and brought to the fore. This is, of course, about living our ideals. But it is also about our health as a living society. Expansive qualities are good for keeping things steady. We need those. But intensive qualities are where evolution is born, and we as the human race need to continue to evolve.

Intensiveness is where the off-the-wall, outlandish, impossible ideas come from. Intensiveness is where things happen that never should have been possible under the old rules. Intensiveness is where rules get broken and limits get surpassed, and one day someone figures out they have wings and the whole animal kingdom is changed forever.

Intensiveness is the skinny branches and the bleeding edge and it is not for everyone, but it is where we change to accommodate the world we live in. It is where the strange and wonderful world of imagination meets reality; it is where our giant brains come in handy, because we can think of things we have never seen.

Intensiveness is the space of innovation.

And the cultures that most nurture, support, and encourage that need to be given the space to lead that process.

The only reason white men dominate the innovation space in the United States is that they are the ones who have hundreds of years of privilege behind them, allowing them to retain some intensive qualities in an expansive system. But all innovators end up spending a lot of time wrestling their way out of the straitjacket of our collective cultural training. And if you're also buried under the weight of four hundred years (or more) of oppression, you might not make it to a place where you can even be seen and heard.

Enough is enough.

This cultural bias has hamstrung us as we moved through the twentieth century and into the twenty-first.

If we lift intensiveness to the same level that expansiveness currently occupies, to be equal with it, our world will change.

I don't know how it will change. But it will almost certainly change for the better.

Think about how you could change your company, your department, your religious community to celebrate intensiveness.

Think about how you could teach differently, move through the world differently, choose differently.

Think about how much energy you *won't* spend trying to suppress yourself.

Once, many years ago, I was serving as a chaplain intern in a large hospital in the near south suburbs of Chicago. Even as interns we took our turns with the on-call shifts, during which time each of us was the only chaplain on duty. One night, I was making my rounds and was suddenly paged to the Emergency Department.

I hurried there to find a family wrestling with the grief of having lost their mother, far too young and completely unexpectedly.

The youngest, her grandchildren, were crying loudly. The husband was crying. But the sister was inconsolable. She was screaming on the floor, clutching her belly, body wracked by great, heaving sobs.

And the hospital didn't know what to do.

Their primary concern was to get them to be quiet.

As a fairly young and inexperienced intern chaplain, I didn't know what to do, but I didn't think the family was the problem. I knew what grief of that magnitude felt like. It felt natural to me that this woman was acting like her heart had been ripped out, because it *had*.

The one room we had for grieving families was tiny, with paper-thin walls.

I could only imagine that as a desperate failure of planning. It's a hospital. People die. That's often a gut-wrenching experience. Of *course* people will make noise. I sat on the floor with the screaming woman, hand on her shoulder. What else could I do?

The nurses told me the family would have to be quiet or leave.

I tried. I don't remember the outcome.

But the family was Black.

And I'm *sure* that affected the hospital's choices.

Our culturally embedded racism is so closely interwoven with culturally embedded anti-intensiveness that it's hard to see the line. Not all intensives outwardly express our intense feelings, but mostly that's about training. We are all born wanting to express what we feel; what varies is how intensely we feel it. Intensives feel intensely.

If we can pivot our behavior to equalize expansive and intensive qualities, our formerly closed institutions will see a vast opening of possibility. "The most segregated hour in North America"—church on Sunday morning—will start to shift.

I recently attended the ordination of a friend and colleague. This colleague has a diverse group of friends and supporters, including some who are part of the Black church tradition.

After the service, one of the participants said that she wanted to shout out her agreement in the middle of the sermon, as her tradition does, but she made herself stay quiet because she wasn't in a Black church, she was in a small Unitarian Universalist church in midcoast Maine.

There in the corner of the robing room we had a long conversation, the preacher and this participant and I, about how we all loved that tradition, how we would have been delighted if she had shouted, and how, because this particular tradition is actively trying to be more flexible, she probably would have started a cascade of other people responding, too.

We have been trained to be quiet and shy, but many of us have a giddy intensive side that, when told it's okay, says, "*Really?* I can *do* that?"

Preaching is not meant to be a one-way process. You know you've got it right when people start singing back. But that's not something supported by our white-British-laden history. Or our present— as recently as 2015, there have been noise complaints about a church in a neighborhood because *the choir was practicing*. It was a Black church. In a neighborhood that was slowly turning white, gentrifying, becoming more reflective of the dominant culture and its norms.

As a minister, this boggles my mind.

No loud singing.

I guess they never read the section of the Bible that talks about singing and dancing.

This is a classic example of dominant culture repressing intensiveness. This is what happens when the people who are used to having the world bend to suit them move into a place that is already occupied by intensives. They try to snuff them out.

It happens with neighborhoods. It happens with schools. Intensity scares people, because they have never been taught to love it in themselves. They don't know what to do with *feelings* and *ideas* and *inspiration*, so they box them up and shut them down. It's hard to blame them; they are as steeped in the tradition as anyone else.

If you are intensive and also Black, expressing it can get you killed, the police have been trained to see intensity expressed as power, and they are very nervous about power they can't control.

Your loved ones will teach you to be very careful how and where you feel. For once, they're right. Intensity *is* power.

It is life force. It is transformation in concentrated form.

But here's the truth: It is *everywhere*. Intensity is in *every single person*. Some got more. Some got less. Some got so much that we call ourselves intensives.

Some only feel it on Christmas morning.

If you're not an intensive, think of that bubbling-up excitement of your birthday when you're a little kid, or the way you felt last winter when you stepped out your front door and spring was finally here. If you're pagan, think of Beltane, when there's so much feeling you're going to burst. Think of losing someone you love deeply. Think of the grief and rage you have about injustice—but not just any injustice, the one that makes you want to scream at the top of your lungs and then march on the White House.

Think of how fiercely you love your child and how you would do anything for them.

Think of a love so deep it is without end.

For me, intensiveness leads me to God.

It gives me the depth of understanding I need to grasp utterly unconditional love.

Intensiveness is the biggest, vastest part of you. The part that you're afraid to let out sometimes. The part that you have to keep quiet sometimes.

What if you didn't?

Imagine a culture where we just *work with* our differences and use them where they can be of most service. *Imagine.*

Imagine a world where we teach to different learning styles, with silent and reflective activities for introverts and talkative interactions for the extroverts, and invite the intensives to do what intensives do best: innovate, transform, challenge, risk. Where intensives are invited to be their excited selves. Where they're given a cave to dive into thinking about something nonstop for a week and then present their results to the expansives, who can think about implementation details built on that framework.

Imagine if, when someone says, "This isn't going far enough," we think immediately that they're probably right?

Imagine that singing out and calling out our agreement is normal.

Imagine that we just plan for people to be so deep in their feelings that it will take a minute to get to the point.

Imagine we have to leave space for spontaneity in our scheduling, which means we only do half as many things but we do them twice as deep.

And what if we sometimes do the impossible, and twice on Sundays?

Because that's what intensives do best.

We are the standard-bearers of grit and determination and fierce fights and brilliant, unthinkable successes.

Our world could use more of that.

Let's bring back wild and radical ideas.

Let's bring back singing and dancing.

Let's bring back retreats that are actually retreats, weeklong immersions into the subject at hand.

And then let's come out into the light and share what we find. Even if it sounds crazy.

Because our history of suppression, colonization, imperialism, and genocide isn't working any longer. In fact, it never did. Contemporary dominant US and Canadian (DUSCAN) culture[1] is the result of colonization, imperialism, and genocide. That's not hyperbole;

---

1   I'm going to refer to US and Canadian culture as a single monolith here. I'm well aware that neither country has just one culture and that the US and Canada have differences. But the particular part of the dominant culture to which I will be referring is fairly consistent. I do not use "North American" because that would include Mexico, which is in a very different category.

it's the truth.

Contemporary DUSCAN culture is also the result of wave after wave of immigration.

When we talk about cultural rearrangement around the world, the lines get very fuzzy very fast. Who's an immigrant? Who's a refugee? Who was taken from their homeland against their will, who left under dire circumstances but under their own power, who paid for their passage with servitude or enslavement, who had rights once they got there, who did not?

Who became whom, when, and what happened if and when they gained traction?

Who got to blend in after six generations?

Who remained a stranger?

Who decided who was a stranger and who wasn't?

These are complicated questions. But when we look at the overall picture of the genocide and repopulation of the United States and Canada, we see that some people were here; some other people arrived here and nearly obliterated the first people and their cultures; and then the new people set up governance and authority that was designed to keep them in power. And so when the *next* new people came, they didn't wipe out the existing system. They came in under it.

They were subject to it.

And eventually, some of them were accepted and some weren't, depending on a variety of factors.

And then there were more new people.

And more and more.

And the system relied on existing structures to oppress each one in turn, and to elevate slightly the ones who came before, mostly.

But with the 20/20 hindsight of five hundred or so years of the continued unfolding of history, we can look back. We can see patterns from here that we couldn't see from there, or didn't know to look for, or chose to ignore.

With the current controversies over admitting Muslim refugees to the United States, the pattern comes into sharp focus. There are things that dominant DUSCAN culture claims not to like, over and over again.

"They" are loud. They're enthusiastic. They like to enjoy themselves. They have large gatherings. They dance. They sing. They have big feelings that are publicly visible. They use tools of worship that the dominant culture doesn't understand.

They are more intensive than we are and it makes us uncomfortable. Make them stop.

Because that is often the price you pay for entering a foreign country, mostly, they do stop. They don't teach their kids the traditions from the home country, because they want their kids to fit in. They learn to make bland peanut butter and jelly with the crusts cut off. They figure out how not to rock the boat.

Because upper crust British culture is one of the most expansive on the planet, and Britain power holders defined "civilization" for hundreds of years. Expansives see civilization very differently from the way intensives might, if left to our own devices. Expansives are the ones who feel that calm, cool, collected behavior is the definition of civilized. Expansives are the ones who feel that feelings should be moderated in public, that food should be inoffensive to everyone, that celebrations should be quiet with clinking glasses.

The country dances and wild fairs, the pagan rituals and traditions, the fierce warriors clad in nothing but woad…they were all dominated by English imperialism, too.

I'm very fond of English and England, but this is the legacy of the Empire on which the sun never set.

We almost—but not quite—lost a lot of very important cultural legacies.

Almost.

But the thing about intensives is, we're fierce. Look at the legacies of intensive cultures and you'll find story after story of reluctant and resistant submission, surrender only to avoid extinction, keeping the stories going underground as a single cultural narrative took over literally half the world. People whose spirits are high are really, really hard to oppress.

So you take away their unique languages. You take away their dances. You take away their music. You take away their soul food. You give them yours, even though it makes them miserable. *Especially* because it makes them miserable. This is the structure of *oppression*, not the structure of Anglos or Saxons or Celts. The lords and ladies feast at the table and drink into the night while they complain that the serfs want to do the same thing. But in the case of the world explorers-*cum*-oppressors, it became a cultural tool to keep everyone down, in place, and too depressed to revolt.

It works, taking away the joy things.

They stop.

They stop everything.

I'd like to say that this all happened a long time ago and it's over now, but that would be bullshit, and anyone who speaks English probably knows that.

It's still happening.

People are *still* doing it.

We have a dream, but we're not there yet.

Some people don't care, or don't think there's anything they can do. Then there are the rest of us. And here's where the dominance of expansive culture comes into play.

Every culture, like every institution and every individual, falls somewhere on the intensive-expansive scale. That doesn't change the ratios of people much—people are still going to be mostly expansive, some intensive. But it will change the way they show up in the world. Intensives will be more free to express themselves in an intensive culture; expansives will feel pressure to act more intensive than they are. Indian culture, for example, is intensive. People are loud, smells are strong, flavors are stronger, people live close together, families fight loudly and make up fiercely. You can see it in its opposite, too—while regular spiritual practice is incense and chanting and bells and festivals and dancing, spiritual elevation in Hinduism involves being more quiet, more withdrawn, more even-tempered—more expansive. Expansiveness is different from everyday life.

Robot Hugs has an excellent webcomic about a phenomenon called "tone policing." (http://www.robot-hugs.com/tone-policing/). Broadly, tone policing involves addressing the emotional tone of a statement or conversation instead of the content as a way of derailing or sidetracking from the original point.

Tone policing is often a way of talking about expansives asking or telling intensives to be more expansive. Expansives operate from a place of profound privilege. They are so used to holding power and having the "right" way be their way that they can't even *tell* when they're exercising privilege. That's how privilege works, of course.

This nation was built on principles of diversity and inclusion, and then we started failing our own ideals right out of the gate.

There is nothing wrong with being loud.

There is nothing wrong with being emotional.

There is nothing wrong with getting angry, or kissing in the middle of the street. Just ask the French.

There's nothing wrong with intensives. There's nothing wrong with intensiveness. And until we come to understand that on a global scale and incorporate it into our leadership expectations from, the boardroom to the Oval Office, we are going to stay a racist society.

It's time for things to shift.

It's time for the learning to go both ways.

It's time for exuberance to have a place at the United Nations, for fierceness to have a place in the Oval Office, for us to teach our intensive kids how to be intensives in public, in leadership, in negotiations, without hurting themselves or anyone else.

Pretending intensives are wrong, or medicating the crap out of them, is not helping anyone.

We need the fires lit.

We need the ideas, the brilliance, the possibility, the risk-taking, the joy.

It's possible to be a healthy adult, a healthy institution, or a healthy country and be an intensive.

But no one is talking about it.

Intensives have been silenced by generations of expansive-dominated leadership under DUSCAN culture, and that's becoming a problem.

What happens when we learn to love and accept the variety of ways that we act--just like we love and accept the variety of ways that we learn (visual/auditory/kinesthetic), or socialize (introvert/extrovert), or give and receive love (the five love languages).

What happens when we recognize the skills and gifts that come with intensiveness AND expansiveness and celebrate both in our cultural and leadership spaces? What happens when we celebrate them in our religious spaces?

Race and cultural barriers aren't about what it feels like to get your heart broken or to fall in love. Race and cultural barriers aren't about what hunger is or how it feels when you don't have a place to sleep. Race and cultural barriers aren't about love or loyalty or strength. Race and cultural barriers show up when we miss each other in the communication relay race. Race and cultural barriers show up when we feel displaced, unheard, not accepted, invisible, rejected. Intensiveness is part of that. How intensive can people be? If you're a minority community, that might be the thing that makes it hardest to get out. If you're a dominant community, that might be the thing that makes it hardest to get in.

This world is going to be a better place.

But it's going to be a better place because everyone with even an ounce of power is going to start moving it in that direction, not because we all dug in and waited for someone to come to us. If you've got power in North America, you've figured out how to play the game. And you can change it for someone else. Stand up for someone. Learn more. Look for the places where intensives could use some more wiggle room and make it.

And if you don't have power, not even an ounce, maybe this frame-work can help you find the places where you can get a toehold. If you're intensive, look for places where you can use your gifts freely and be yourself.

5 – 2
INTERCULTURAL CONFLICT STYLES AND INTENSIVES

A few summers ago I co-taught a class at a retreat center with my friend and colleague Tamara Lebak, who at the time was a minister serving a church down in Oklahoma. During that class I was introduced to the Intercultural Conflict Style Inventory. It's complex and beautiful; if you haven't taken the it, I highly recommend it. This inventory is striking because its four-quadrant system puts all the different conflict/cultural styles on even footing as equally valid. We tend to have some ideas about what constitutes the right way to interact, and the inventory strips that out and says, instead, that every way is the right way; it just depends what your culture is.

At the risk of oversimplifying, the four possibilities of cultural habit are:

1. Loud and direct;

2. Loud and indirect;

3. Quiet and direct; and

    4. Quiet and indirect.

Those four styles have some correlation with intensive and expansive self-expression, although it doesn't correlate exactly—you can't say that all Italians are this or all Indians are that. Some Italians are expansive, some Indians are, too; some British are intensive.

Here's an example of how intercultural (intensive-expansive) communication might look.

We need to know each other, and we need each other. The art of functioning with mixed intensiveness levels in a group is a question of trust. For expansives, expression doesn't come as easily, and it tends to be more muted. An expansive is more likely to say, "Well, I'm feeling a little sad," while an intensive with the same level of sorrow is likely to be crying.

In expansive culture, somebody says, "How are you doing?" and you say, "I'm fine." If you don't know them, you don't tell them you're sad. You don't know what they're going to do with that information, and they're not really asking. What they're really asking is, "Can I make a brief and superficial connection with you while I'm checking out your groceries?" "Sure, you can do that. I'm fine." But most people can tell when they look at you if you're not fine. So then the conventions of the culture have actually forced you into a ritualized lie. We agree to the lie, but it does create distance and disconnection.

Less trust and less connection allows people to feel like they don't have to do anything challenging, but it also keeps people feeling alone. Feeling connected is vulnerable; *being* connected is even more vulnerable. Telling the truth about yourself is a challenge in our culture because we do it so seldom, and only in certain contexts. I was lucky to grow up Unitarian Universalist in a place and at a time when its youth culture was actively teaching and living a kind of radical honesty. I learned how to tell the truth about myself a little bit in my adolescence in southwestern Connecticut in the 1990s. I carried a little piece of that culture to college, where I found a group of people who behaved the same way. A few years after I left college I ran across another community that was working on some skills similar to those I had honed, so I hopped from subculture to subculture looking for places where I could be myself as I had learned to be when I was in high school. This process was incredibly nourishing for me. It is also proving incredibly useful, because I want to live in a world where we trust each other and I think the way to build that world is to walk around like I trust people.

I recognize the limits of social interaction—I don't tell my whole story to the grocery checker—but if someone asks how I am, the five-second appropriate-to-somebody-I-don't-know-and-I'm-not-going-to-be-with-for-very-long answer is "I've had better days" or "I'm not having a great day." Sometimes I add, "At least it's almost over; I'm looking forward to tomorrow." I don't make it their problem; I just tell them.

When you strive for a modicum of emotional transparency, given other people's boundaries and comfort levels, it becomes an opportunity for your own growth. When you're truthful about what you're feeling, you start to inquire of yourself what you're *actually feeling*. It changes things. You become more self-aware, because that information becomes useful to you. If you never need to know how you feel, you don't have to ask how you feel—and you get out of the habit of asking. But when you work your way through it, it influences how you interact with the world, it influences what you tell people, and that level of awareness changes things. It's like an electron: once you start looking at it, it moves. You can't shine a light on it and expect it to stay in the same place. That kind of self-awareness is not just useful for intensives, it's actively rewarding. Expansives, on the other hand, might be okay with less information.

If we want to become truly balanced, we have to move intensiveness toward the center, probably by widening the Overton Window—the range of ideas that the public will accept. Expansives and intensives as cultural functioning models need to be equally valid. Right now that window is way over to the expansive side of the scale.

If we do not trust the person we're talking to, then it becomes important for us to hide what we feel because knowing what we truly feel means that they have a piece of information that they can use against us. But *the minute we decide we're all here to serve the best interests of everyone involved, showing what you feel becomes an asset.*

Showing what you feel builds trust; hiding what you feel drives the power imbalance. We need to live in a world that's more trust-oriented and less imbued with power imbalance.

When we stop trying to gain the upper hand and start trying to build community, it completely changes the behavioral matrix we need. If I know you're angry or hurt or delighted, that makes it easier for me to hurt you, sure, but it also makes it easier for me to *please* you. If you assume that I want to make your life better, then all of a sudden the best thing you can do is be angry when you're angry and be hurt when you're hurt. It doesn't matter whether I'm the one you're angry at; what matters is that you can tell me that you're feeling angry, so I can figure out—*with* you—how to alleviate the situation. You have to believe I'm with you, not against you. That's important.

Being able to translate across the lines of emotional style, to move fluidly between them, to honor all the points on the continuum from intensiveness to expansiveness, will really change the way we are with each other in the world. It changes intimacy, changes relationships, it changes our lives. We are never going to be the same.

5 – 3

CONCLUSION: BUILDING THE BRIDGE

I wrote this book to change us—to change all of us. I wrote this book to change the way we think about the people we see and the people we know. I wrote this book to change the way that we feel about being uncomfortable, because it needs to change. In expansive cultural space we're supposed to be okay with being slightly uncomfortable all the time, but we're not supposed to talk about it. Let's talk about it. Let's name it. Let's name it without judgment, and let's not take responsibility for other people's experiences. We care about each other, but let's find out how we can act with caring without having to change the core of who we are.

Expressing your feelings should be respectable; expressing your feelings loudly should be respectable; expressing your feelings quietly should be respectable; choosing not to express your feelings should also be respectable. (This is a hard one for intensives, because we tend to not understand why people won't just say what they feel.)

If you don't want to say what you're feeling, try saying, "I would rather not share that." "I'm not comfortable saying so." "I pass."

This is not meant as a strategy for keeping yourself safe, but the reverse. We need to stop keeping ourselves safe. Safety by silence is a lie.

Isolation does not keep us safe, and that's one of the lessons we need to learn from intensive cultures. There is nothing safe about being alone. The damage from isolation is so bad that newborn children who do not have community die, even if they have all of their other physical needs met—even if they get food and water and they are kept warm, they die from lack of touch. They die from lack of human contact. *They die.* We are not meant to be alone, we are not meant to be isolated, and when we allow intensive culture to teach us that we need to be connected, it changes everything.

Even telling someone that you don't want to tell them something is connecting. When intensive culture penetrates deeply enough into an environment, people start to express themselves in such a way that they end up more connected. There is connection to be had in shared living, in shared experience, in quietly brushing up against other lives. An expansive culture really values that part; intensive culture asks for more.

While not everybody's going to adopt "more," everybody has the opportunity to learn what that would mean—to learn those tools, to have them available when you're feeling separated. Be honest when you're feeling separated; be vulnerable when you're feeling separated; let your feelings show when you're feeling separated— not just the anger, not just the anger that comes from unmet needs or fear. Anger that comes from unmet needs is fine, but what the person across from you needs to know is: *What is the need?* That's where intensive culture really shines, because it encourages us to set aside feeling safe and say what we're really feeling.

Underneath the anger is something else. Underneath the anger is *I'm scared.* I'm scared of losing something; I'm scared of not get- ting something; or I'm scared of getting hurt; I'm scared of being abandoned; I'm scared of being alone. It's primal fears that drive the anger. *I'm scared of not being safe* can drive the anger that drives a war. *I'm scared of change*: What happens if I lose my position of power in the system? *I'm scared I won't belong anywhere anymore?* That's the fear of loss of community, identity, self.

An expansive won't always want to go that deep. That's okay. Even intensives have limits. But to know that it's available, and to be able to access it as a tool, is to know that you aren't trapped. And not being trapped can be the difference between life and death.

Many of our society's problems with sexism seem to be a direct result of that fear. Our culture, like many others, has told men exactly where they belong and what they're supposed to do for a very long time. If you take that structure and direction away, then how do they know where do they belong? Is there even a place for them? They get angry because they're *allowed* to get angry—it's often the only tool they've been given. Without other feelings, though, they never get to the underlying need. Intensive culture at least gives us the tools to start asking those questions.

Because I'm promoting intensive inclusion so heavily here, I have to keep saying this: there's nothing wrong with expansive culture. It's just that it's been the dominant culture for a long time now, and we're out of balance. That needs to change. This expansive-biased culture isn't providing answers to some critical questions at this juncture in our maturation of the universe, and we need a different approach.

Expansives don't necessarily come naturally to the same kinds of expression that intensives do, but there's no reason why expansives can't use the tools of intensiveness. Expansive *culture* is different from expansive *individuals*. Many expansive individuals are totally comfortable saying what they feel—they just say it in a very moderate and low-key way. In the name of cross-cultural communication, intensives need to learn to take that seriously. If an expansive says, "Well, I'm feeling a little angry right now," that might be the equivalent of an intensive shouting at the top of their lungs, and we need to receive that information with the same gravity. This is what codeswitching looks like for us.

Expansives are not incapable of saying what they feel. It's expansive cultural domination that has limited our ability to honor that in large-scale spaces—in institutions in national and international relations. Think of Khrushchev thumping his shoe on the table at the UN—that was an intensive who knew he couldn't be intensive in that space and finally exploded. Being in a mixed cultural space where intensiveness and expansiveness are equally valued, equally honored, equally accepted, equally legitimate will mean that people have to learn to code such intensive gestures as legitimate and simultaneously hear quiet expressions of emotion as important.

It's time to not just move ourselves from not having intensives present to having intensives present, it's actually *time for us to move from privileging expansiveness to bringing intensiveness equal with expansiveness.* We need to move from tolerance to appreciation, and we need to do it fast. We're losing people and cultures and connections faster than we can track them.

What does this mean in terms of world peace? Let me back up a step.

When a culture privileges a specific behavior or set of behaviors, that becomes what it takes to get ahead. So in our dominant culture here in the US, what it takes to get ahead is conforming to that dominant behavioral paradigm, which is expansive.

Here's what that looks like: We sit quietly, we're very polite, we do what we're told. If we disagree with someone, we disagree quietly, politely. We don't shout—in fact we try really hard not to have very intense feelings, at least not in public. We marginalize and ostracize emotion, self-expression, color, movement, feeling. Or we confine it to sports and art. Intense feelings are not generally considered suitable for public display. When Justin Trudeau took office as prime minister in 2015, an editorial in one of Canada's major newspapers complained that he kissed his wife too much in public and it was making the writer uncomfortable. I don't know if Prime Minister Trudeau is an intensive, but expecting someone not to display their feelings in public is a very expansive cultural bias.

Dominant culture isn't going anywhere—the dominant culture is this expansive style culture and it's not changing. But if you look around the pocket immigrant communities, in the pocket minority communities around the country, you'll find that intensiveness has been flourishing there right along, until it scares someone.

We have to know who we are serving and who we are trying to serve. We have to know who we're interacting with and who we want to be interacting with.

We have to know what we're giving the world and what we *want* to be giving the world.

Because whether you run a business or a religious institution or a household, or if you just participate in any of those things, you are giving something to the world.

You are adding something to the world.

You are bringing content and experiences to the world.

And if you're going to bring content and experiences to the world, it helps to know what you're trying to do.

If you're an intensive like me, you do it first and analyze it later. If you're expansive, you probably have a five-year plan.

You are giving the world something.

You are contributing to the world.

If it's not going the way you want it to, if you're frustrated because you don't have more diversity or more connections or whatever it is, try this lens. see what it does for you.

Because when we build this bridge the world changes.

When we build this bridge we change the world.

RESOURCES

If you'd like more information about the material in this book:

The website is http://yourenottoomuch.com/. It includes all of the current resources I've created. These include:

- Facebook group for intensives

- A parents-of-intensives kit

- My Patreon site, where you can sign up to get access to material too new for the book

- YouTube videos

- Podcasts, sermon recordings, and other audio files

- Coaching/consulting/speaking information

- Press resources

- The full-length, computer-scored assessment

What I do: you can hire me to come to you or work with you remotely. I offer coaching, consulting, and speaking services, and am happy to talk with you about what you might need for you or your organization. I also offer VIP days, which are in-person full immersion workdays, and workshops for groups and organizations.

ACKNOWLEDGEMENTS

I don't know how I can possibly make a list of everyone who has been part of this, and I'm desperately afraid of forgetting someone, but I feel like I have to try. Writing this book has been such an act of desperate love. I couldn't not create it. But I also couldn't have done it without all these people.

So many grateful thanks:

To my editor, Sarah Grey, who read it the first time and said so many nice things about it that I had to believe her even when I had my doubts, and for her sweet opinions, flexibility, and stories about her intensive kid.

To my parents, for providing financial support even though they didn't know what they were supporting.

To Sarah, Sarah, Heather, Megan, Michelle, Janine, and Aife, and others, for supporting various parts of the project and the tours, for reading and believing in this work, and for going out on a limb to promote me through their networks.

To Catherine, for advance reading and effusive support.

To Natasha, for her last-minute design skills.

To everyone who came to my workshops and listened to my talks as I was refining this work.

To my close clergy colleagues, and especially the FOWH colleagues; you ensure that I do not forget that this is a ministry.

To my coaching colleagues, who keep me moving forward and hold spaces big enough for me to grow into.

To the Sex Geek Summer Camp people, for being a kickass community of entrepreneurs who are creative and unstoppable.

To the Boom Brigade, for being a place where bigness thrives, and to Fabeku, the fearless leader.

To the people in my life who have kept me alive long enough to learn all these things and do this work, and who have taught me about the workings of their own heads by letting me know them.

To my dear friends, too many to name; this could be a whole page just of you.

To Lara, you are always a candle in the darkness.

ABOUT THE AUTHOR

Leela Sinha is a Unitarian Univeralist minster who studied at
Carleton College and Meadville/Lombard Theological School.
In addition, she has trained at The Coaches Training Institute, The
Green Mountain Institute, and the International House of Reiki.
Her experiences and observations from years of work with people
in a broad variety of contexts as community minister, coach, speak-
er, consultant, and bodyworker led to the development of the SIEF
Framework. She lives on the coast of Maine with her two cats.

59146298R00209

Made in the USA
Charleston, SC
27 July 2016